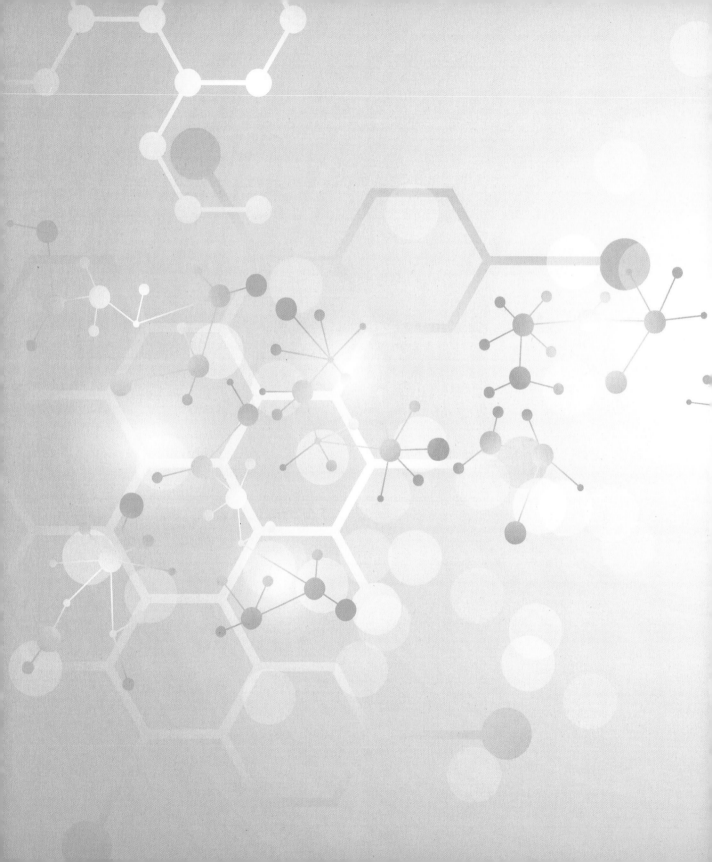

STEVE
SPANGLER'S
super cool
SCIENCE
EXPERIMENTS
for kids!

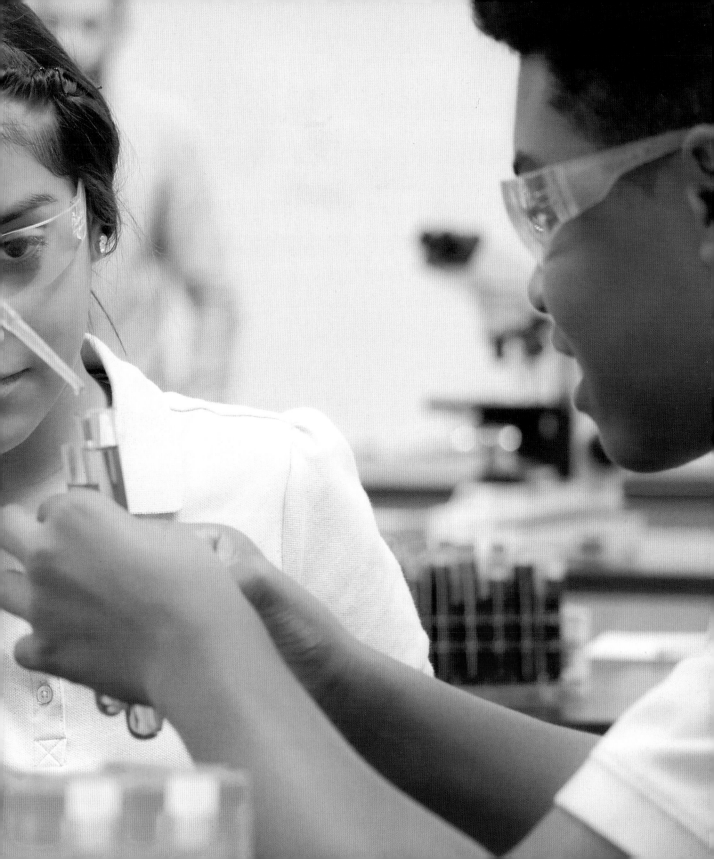

SCIENCE
A NEVER-ENDING QUEST FOR KNOWLEDGE!

Have you ever wanted to understand why oil and water don't mix, how your lungs take in air or how rockets blast through space? With science, you can discover the forces at work throughout the known universe! In each of these 50 experiments, you'll have a front-row seat to understanding a little bit more about the world around you. So put on your thinking caps and prepare to make some incredible discoveries!

BETTER THAN MAGIC

Science Supplies

Although most of these experiments call for common household objects, you may need to stock up on ¼"-20 hex nuts (you can find these inexpensively at your local hardware store) and disposable pipettes (found online or at a local craft store).

ALWAYS ASK WHY!

WE LIVE IN AN INFINITELY FASCINATING WORLD. From the way light refracts in a bubble to the way crystals form deep in the Earth to the movement of the planets in the cosmos, life is teeming with endless discoveries if you know where to look. Or, better yet, what to ask!

Every great scientist didn't just wake up one morning, kick off their bedsheets and shout, "THAT'S IT! I get it now!" and go on their merry way being famous for knowing things. Instead, something even more remarkable happened: Each and every one of them observed something that sparked their curiosity about wonders big and small, and they began asking questions, like, "Why is the sky blue?" "Why do apples fall from trees?" "How does the Earth rotate, and what exactly is it rotating around?" "Do I exist?" (OK, that's Descartes territory, but I digress.)

The point being, every great thinker you can think of—Galileo, Newton, Darwin, Mendel, Einstein, Tesla, Sagan, Hawking and a host of other bright minds—began their journeys with a single step. And with any of these 50 experiments, you can start down your own winding path to discovering just how incredible the world around us truly is. This book is packed to the brim with fun science activities, demonstrations, nifty head-scratching tricks and science fair projects guaranteed to wow a crowd and get you hooked on learning. And the best part? Just about all of them can be done using materials you already have at home! But just because you can find some of these items in your kitchen, garage or medicine cabinet doesn't mean they can't reveal some of the mysteries of the universe with a bang, fizz, pop or all-out explosion of color!

Keep asking "how" and "why" and let the wonder of science lead you on your own amazing adventure!

—STEVE SPANGLER

SCIENCE SAFETY

Science is loads of fun, but there are a few things you need to keep in mind when you set out to conduct an experiment. What makes these activities exciting—knives, fire, eruptions and other cool stuff—are the same things that amp up the danger factor. That's why you need to prep your space (or "lab") with safety in mind before you begin any experiment.

1. ALWAYS ASK AN ADULT.

Before you start any science experiment, ask your parent or guardian if it's OK. Even if you aren't going to work with anything particularly dangerous, it's best to get permission before you stock up on supplies. You should definitely have an adult's help if an experiment calls for using a sharp blade or drill, heating substances or lighting something on fire.

2. READ ALL INSTRUCTIONS.

This is the only way to ensure you have everything you need for the experiment, that you understand what will happen whether or not it goes as planned, and that you stay safe.

DURING ANY EXPERIMENT, ALWAYS KEEP LONG HAIR TIED BACK AND WEAR CLOSED-TOE SHOES.

3. WEAR PROTECTIVE CLOTHING, IF NECESSARY.

Wear safety glasses when working with anything that shatters, bubbles, pops or explodes. You'll also want to wear heavy gloves when working with hot objects.

4. WASH YOUR HANDS AFTER YOU'RE DONE EXPERIMENTING...

You don't want anything lingering on your skin after completing your research.

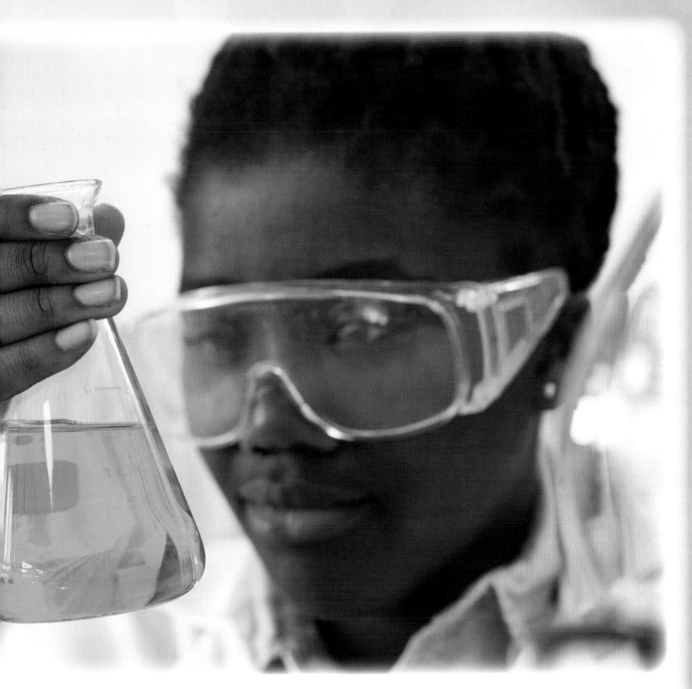

5. ...AND DON'T TOUCH YOUR MOUTH OR EYES.

This is always sound advice in terms of keeping yourself healthy, but you definitely DO NOT want to get anything like vinegar in your eyes!

6. NO EATING OR DRINKING IN THE LAB.

Keep food and drink out of the area where you're conducting your experiment. You don't want to accidentally ingest anything unsafe!

THE SCIENTIFIC METHOD

We use the scientific method to understand how things work. Simply put, it is the best tool we have to determine what is true. Many of the experiments in this book demonstrate concepts scientists know well. But with the scientific method, you can turn these activities into opportunities to explore the forces at work in our world step by step! Here's how it works:

1 ASK A QUESTION

To get started, pick something you want to learn more about. For example, if you do the Amazing 9-Layer Density Tower experiment on page 60, you might find yourself wondering, "How would other materials like a sunflower seed, a poker chip or a small button respond if I dropped them in, too?" Start taking notes about the things you would like to compare.

2 GATHER INFORMATION AND OBSERVE

You'll see this word a lot: "Observe." It's the simplest way to dive in and begin learning about something. To continue the example from before, start to mull those other objects from Step 1 over in your mind a bit, focusing on how you might compare their size, smoothness and weight to the other items you've added to the tower.

3 FORM A HYPOTHESIS

Now that you've spent some time researching your materials, it's time to make an educated guess about how far or how little they will sink in the tower compared to your original items. This is what scientists call a hypothesis. What do you think will happen and why?

A CONSTANT IS A COMPONENT OF A SCIENTIFIC EXPERIMENT THAT IS ALWAYS THE SAME. A **VARIABLE** IS A COMPONENT OF A SCIENTIFIC EXPERIMENT THAT CHANGES.

DRAW YOUR CONCLUSION

6 Once you have the results of your experiment, you can share them with everyone! Write down why you undertook the experiment and what happened. If you aren't sure why something did or did not work as you imagined, do some more research and keep experimenting! Remember: There's always something new to learn.

LET'S EXPERIMENT

4 Get ready for one of the most exciting steps in your scientific journey: testing your hypothesis! Recreate your original experiment using your new materials, but be sure to change only one thing—otherwise known as a variable—at a time. In this case, you're changing the item you drop in the tower. Record your findings.

ANALYZE YOUR RESULTS

5 What happened? Was it what you expected, or did something else occur? It's OK if things did not line up with your hypothesis. The amazing thing about science is that you can always formulate a new hypothesis to test!

BETTER THAN MAGIC

THESE EXPERIMENTS MIGHT LOOK LIKE TRICKS, BUT THEY'RE BASED IN REAL SCIENCE YOU CAN SEE!

See page 30 to make a lemon battery!

LEAK-PROOF BAG

FRUIT-POWERED BATTERY

WORLD'S SIMPLEST MOTOR

SHARPIE® PEN COLOR SCIENCE

USE PERMANENT MARKERS TO CREATE DRAWABLE TIE-DYE!

MATERIALS

Plastic Cup

Rubber Band

91% Isopropyl Alcohol (Rubbing Alcohol)

Sharpie® Pens, Various Colors

Piece of White Cotton Fabric

Dropper Squeeze Bottle (or Eye Dropper)

LET'S EXPERIMENT

1 PLACE the fabric over the mouth of the plastic cup. Position the opening of the cup directly under the section of fabric that you want to decorate. Stretch the rubber band over the fabric and the cup to secure the fabric in place.

2 POUR the rubbing alcohol into the dropper squeeze bottle. Secure the cap. If using an eye dropper, fill it with the rubbing alcohol.

3 USING the pen of your choice, draw dots or circles in the center of the stretched-out fabric. Whatever designs you choose to make, keep this area small—about the size of a quarter. You'll need this room to properly see the colors in the next step. Use another color marker to fill in spaces in between the first shapes.

4

SLOWLY squeeze approximately 20 drops of rubbing alcohol into the center of the circle of dots. DO NOT flood the design area with rubbing alcohol. The key is to drip the rubbing alcohol slowly in the center of the design and gently allow the molecules of ink to bleed outward from the center. Apply as much or as little rubbing alcohol as desired, but do not let the pattern spread beyond the edges of the cup.

Allow the developed design to dry for three to five minutes before moving on to a new area of the fabric.

5 HEAT-SET your design by placing the fabric in a laundry dryer for approximately 15 minutes.

TAKE IT FURTHER

Experiment with various patterns, dot sizes and color combinations. Squares, half circles, wavy lines and polygons all make unique patterns when rubbing alcohol travels across the ink.

HOW DOES IT WORK?

This is a lesson in the concepts of solubility, color mixing and the movement of molecules. The Sharpie® markers contain permanent ink, which will not wash away with water. Permanent ink is hydrophobic, meaning it is not soluble in water. However, the molecules of ink are soluble in another solvent, rubbing alcohol, which carries the different colors of ink with it as it spreads in a circular pattern from the center of the fabric.

Did you know?

RUBBING ALCOHOL IS A VERSATILE HOUSEHOLD ITEM YOU PROBABLY ALREADY HAVE IN YOUR MEDICINE CABINET. IT CAN BE USED AS AN ANTISEPTIC FOR CUTS AND SCRAPES AS WELL AS A DISINFECTANT TO CLEAN EVERYTHING FROM DRY ERASE BOARDS TO JEWELRY TO ELECTRONICS AND MORE!

LEAK-PROOF BAG

POINTY PENCILS ARE NO MATCH FOR POLYMERS!

MATERIALS

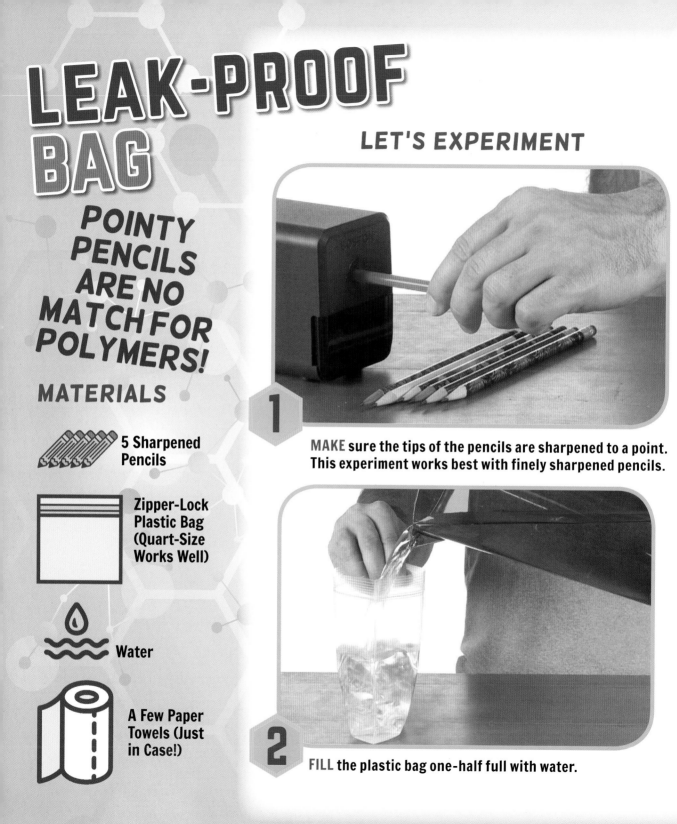

5 Sharpened Pencils

Zipper-Lock Plastic Bag (Quart-Size Works Well)

Water

A Few Paper Towels (Just in Case!)

LET'S EXPERIMENT

1 MAKE sure the tips of the pencils are sharpened to a point. This experiment works best with finely sharpened pencils.

2 FILL the plastic bag one-half full with water.

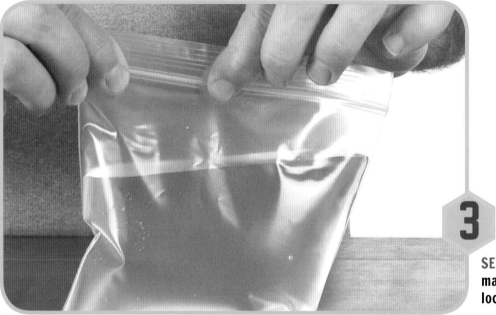

3

SEAL the bag shut, making sure the zipper lock is secure.

4

YOU MAY want to try this over a sink, or have a few paper towels handy just in case: Hold a pencil in one hand and the top of the bag in the other hand. Slowly push a pencil through one side of the bag and partway out the other.

Believe it or not, you can do this without spilling a drop! The long chains of molecules that make up the bag seal back around the pencil and prevent water from leaking out.

LEAK-PROOF BAG

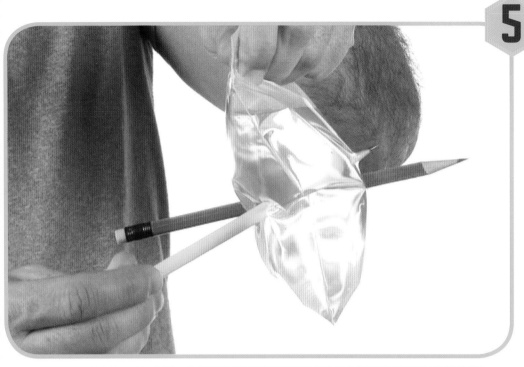

5

GENTLY push a second pencil through the bag.

NOTE: Be careful not to push the pencils all the way through the holes or your science magic trick will quickly turn into a "clean-it-up" activity.

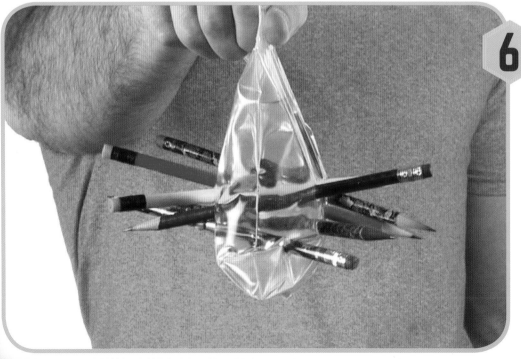

6

SEE how many pencils you can fit!

When you are finished, hold the bag over the sink or a bucket and remove the pencils, then toss the bag in the recycling bin and dry the pencils.

TAKE IT FURTHER

Try experimenting with plastic bags and pencils of different thicknesses and sizes. The thicker the bag, the harder it is to get the pencil to pass through. For a really thin bag, use a plastic bag from the produce section of the grocery store. Which type of pencil works best—a round one or one with edges?

HOW DOES IT WORK?

The zipper-lock plastic bag you used was most likely made out of a polymer called low-density polyethylene (LDPE), one of the most widely used packaging materials in the world. LDPE is low in cost, lightweight, durable, a barrier to moisture and very flexible.

Think of the polyethylene molecules as long strands of freshly cooked spaghetti—the tip of the sharpened pencil can easily slip between and push apart the flexible strands of spaghetti, but the strands' flexible property helps to form a temporary seal against the edge of the pencil. When the pencil is removed, the hole in the plastic bag remains because the polyethylene molecules were pushed aside permanently, and the water leaks out.

Did you know?

ALTHOUGH PLASTIC BAGS ARE USED FOR AN AVERAGE OF 12 MINUTES, IT CAN TAKE BETWEEN 500 AND 1,000 YEARS FOR A SINGLE BAG TO DEGRADE IN A LANDFILL.

SPINNING MATCH

GIVE THIS TABLE TRICK A WHIRL USING STATIC ELECTRICITY.

MATERIALS

Clear Plastic Cup

Matchstick

2 Nickels

Balloon

LET'S EXPERIMENT

1

LAY one nickel flat on a table. Carefully balance the second nickel vertically on top of the flat nickel.

2

BALANCE a matchstick on top of the vertical nickel.

3

BEING careful not to bump your balanced apparatus, gently place the plastic cup over the matchstick and nickels.

4

BLOW UP and tie off a balloon. Rub the balloon against your shirt, hair or carpet to generate some static electricity.

5

MANEUVER the balloon around the outside of the cup—the match follows the balloon!

TAKE IT FURTHER

Try changing the amount of time you take to rub the balloon or switching up the objects you rub the balloon against to give it static electricity. How far away can you move the balloon from the cup and still get the match to spin?

Did you know?

ALTHOUGH MATCHES AS WE KNOW THEM TODAY ARE LARGELY A PRODUCT OF 19TH-CENTURY INNOVATION, ACCORDING TO THE ROMAN POET MARTIAL, CRUDE SULFUR MATCHES OR SULPHURATA WERE USED BY THE ROMANS AS FAR BACK AS THE FIRST CENTURY.

HOW DOES IT WORK?

This experiment revolves around static electricity. When you rub the balloon on a coarse surface such as your shirt, hair or carpet, you give the balloon additional electrons, generating a negative static charge. The match, meanwhile, has a neutral charge. When an object has a negative charge, it repels the electrons of other objects and attracts that object's protons. When the neutrally charged object is light enough, like the match in this case, the negatively charged object will attract the lightweight object. But if you try attracting a match while it's laying on a table, it doesn't work. Why? You must reduce the amount of friction acting on the match for this experiment to work, which is why you balance the match on the rim of a nickel. Balancing the match enables less surface area to be directly affected by friction, which enables the match to rotate more freely.

MYSTERY BALLOON POP

CAN SUNLIGHT ALONE POP A BALLOON?

MATERIALS

Clear Balloon

Black Balloon

Magnifying Glass

Sunlight

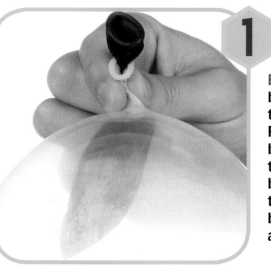

1

BLOW UP the clear balloon, but don't tie off the end! Partially insert the black balloon into the inflated clear balloon. Make sure the opening to the black balloon is still accessible.

2

BLOW UP the black balloon until it is about half the size of the clear balloon, then tie off the black balloon.

PUSH the inflated black balloon the rest of the way into the clear balloon. Tie off the clear balloon.

3

4 USE the magnifying glass to focus sunlight on the black balloon inside. The black balloon pops!

HOW DOES IT WORK?

When you use a magnifying glass to focus the sun's rays into a dot, you create a spot that is incredibly hot. With the clear balloon, most of the light and heat pass right through the balloon's surface. Since the clear balloon is nearly transparent, the same thing happens when it is exposed to light, even in a high concentration, thus it doesn't pop. Black, on the other hand, does not reflect light or heat but absorbs it. The heat absorbed by the black balloon from the focused sunlight quickly causes the bonds of the balloon to weaken until it can no longer contain the air on the inside and eventually explodes.

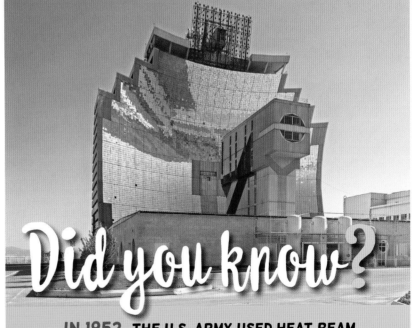

Did you know?

IN 1952, THE U.S. ARMY USED HEAT BEAM TECHNOLOGY TO CREATE A DEVICE CALLED A SOLAR FURNACE, LIKE THE ONE PICTURED ABOVE. COMPOSED OF SOME 200 CURVED MIRRORS, THE FURNACE REACHES TEMPERATURES OF AROUND 6,000 DEGREES FAHRENHEIT, ALLOWING IT TO MELT ROCK.

FLAME LIGHT RELIGHT

WHAT CAUSES THE FLAME TO GO OUT?

⚠️

SAFETY NOTE
Have an adult help you with this experiment!

MATERIALS

Two Graduated Cylinders (or Tall Kitchen Glasses)

Measuring Spoons

Popsicle Stick

Lighter

Hydrogen Peroxide

White Vinegar

Yeast

Baking Soda

Safety Goggles

LET'S EXPERIMENT

1 ADD **1** teaspoon of baking soda and 1 teaspoon of yeast to each of the two graduated cylinders.

2 SHAKE, spin and twirl the graduated cylinders to mix the baking soda and yeast mixture until well combined.

3 ADD a generous splash of hydrogen peroxide to one of the graduated cylinders.

IN THE second graduated cylinder, pour in a generous amount of white vinegar. The addition of hydrogen peroxide and vinegar to their respective cylinders creates a reaction with bubbling and fizzing.

HAVE an adult use a lighter to ignite a popsicle stick. Allow the popsicle stick to burn until you see an ember glowing.

HOLD the lit end of the popsicle stick down into the graduated cylinder with vinegar. (You do not need to touch the bubbles or liquid.) The flame will extinguish.

FLAME LIGHT RELIGHT

NOW, move the still-smoking popsicle stick into the graduated cylinder that contains hydrogen peroxide. (Again, no need to touch the bubbles or liquid in the cylinder.) The ember where a flame once was will begin to glow more intensely until the flame relights!

Repeat placing the popsicle stick into the vinegar graduated cylinder and then the hydrogen peroxide graduated cylinder to watch it extinguish and reignite again and again!

HOW DOES IT WORK?

A fire requires three components (known as the fire triangle or combustion triangle): oxygen, fuel and sufficient heat for the flames to ignite and stay lit. Remove any one of these and the flame will extinguish or "go out." For the popsicle flame, the three necessary components are present during the initial lighting of the fire: the heat generates from a separate flame, the lighter; the wood of the popsicle stick provides the fuel; and the oxygen level in the atmosphere is enough to sustain a flame.

When you hold the flaming popsicle stick in the first graduated cylinder, it extinguishes because one of the three components of the fire triangle is missing. Why? The answer lies in the bubbling mixture in the cylinder. The baking soda (a.k.a. sodium bicarbonate) is a base, while the vinegar (or acetic acid) is a weak acid. Combine the two and the immediate acid-base reaction creates carbonic acid, which is unstable and decomposes into carbon dioxide (CO_2) and water (H_2O). The bubbling you see inside the cylinder is the production of the CO_2 gas. When you dip the popsicle stick into the cylinder, you expose the flame to concentrated CO_2 gas, and the lack of oxygen extinguishes the flame.

After placing the popsicle stick into the second cylinder, however, the ember glows brighter and the flame reignites due to the reintroduction of oxygen (O_2). The high concentration of O_2 in the cylinder makes the heat source become more intense until the flame ignites again.

Hydrogen peroxide (H_2O_2) is fairly unstable and always tries to decompose into water (H_2O) and oxygen (O_2). When yeast is mixed with hydrogen peroxide, it acts as a catalyst to the decomposition. This creates oxygen at a much faster rate, which you can see bubbling inside the cylinder. Placing the partially glowing ember into the concentrated oxygen completes the fire triangle and reignites the flame.

Did you know?

DUE TO OUR PLANET'S UNIQUE OXYGEN LEVELS AMONG THE KNOWN UNIVERSE, EARTH IS THE ONLY CONFIRMED PLANET ON WHICH FIRES BURN.

FRUIT-POWERED BATTERY

BUILD A COMPLETE CIRCUIT USING THE POWER OF CITRUS!

MATERIALS

- 4 Lemons
- 4 Pennies
- 4 Zinc-Galvanized Nails
- 5 Sets of Alligator Clips
- Mini-LED Lights
- Kitchen Knife

LET'S EXPERIMENT

1

USE a kitchen knife to cut a penny-sized slit in all four lemons.

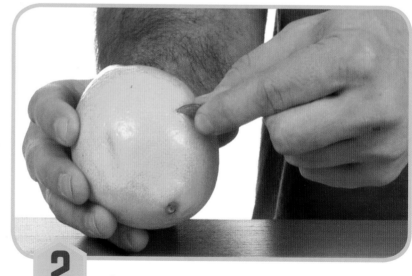

2

INSERT a penny halfway into each of the slits.

3

PUSH a zinc-galvanized nail into each of the lemons, opposite the penny. Don't let the nail and penny touch in or out of the lemon.

4

USING a set of alligator clips, connect a nail in one lemon to a penny in another lemon.

5

CONNECT all four lemons together with alligator clips. Each set of alligator clips should connect a nail to a penny.

FRUIT-POWERED BATTERY

6

CONNECT one of the last alligator clips to the last remaining open penny.

7

CONNECT the remaining clip to the last open nail.

8

ATTACH each of the two loose alligator clips to one leg of the LED. The chemical energy in the lemons powers the LED with electrical energy!

HOW DOES IT WORK?

Batteries comprise two different metals suspended in an acidic solution. In this experiment, the two metals are zinc and copper—the zinc is in the galvanization on the nails, and the pennies are actually copper-plated zinc, while the acid comes from the citric acid inside each lemon.

The two metal components are electrodes, the parts of a battery where electrical current enters and leaves the battery. With a zinc and copper setup, the electrons flow out of the penny (copper) and into the nail (zinc) through the acidic juice inside the lemon. In the exchange of electrons between the zinc and the copper over the acid bridge, copper accepts two electrons from zinc which accounts for the current.

Once the Fruit-Powered Battery is connected to the LED, you've completed a circuit. As the electrical current passes through the LED, it powers the LED and then passes back through all of the lemons before getting to the LED again.

NOTE: LEDs are polar sensitive, meaning they will only glow if the current is flowing through them in the right direction. If the LED doesn't glow the first time, switch the alligator clips attached to its legs and try again.

Did you know?

CITRIC ACID IS ADDED TO CANNED FOODS LIKE MEAT, FRUITS AND VEGETABLES TO PROTECT AGAINST BOTULISM, A SERIOUS ILLNESS CAUSED BY THE HARMFUL CLOSTRIDIUM BOTULINUM BACTERIA THAT OCCURS IN IMPROPERLY STERILIZED PRESERVED FOODS.

PENDULUM CATCH

IT'S A SCIENTIFIC SHOWDOWN OF FRICTION VS. GRAVITY!

MATERIALS

15 Identical Hex Nuts

Cotton String (or a Shoelace or Yarn)

Scissors

LET'S EXPERIMENT

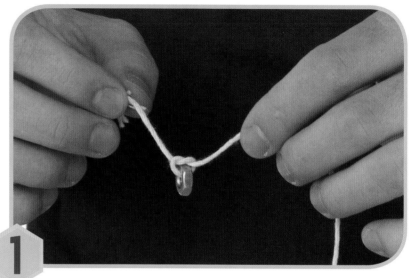

1

THREAD one hex nut onto one end of the string and secure it in place with a knot.

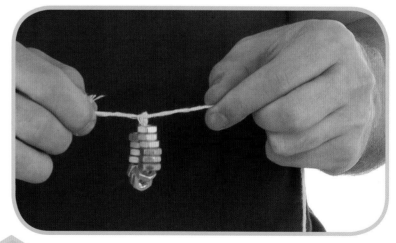

2

THREAD the remaining 14 hex nuts onto the opposite end of the string. Create a small loop by tying the loose end of string right above the stack of hex nuts in a knot, as pictured. This will help keep the hex nuts in place.

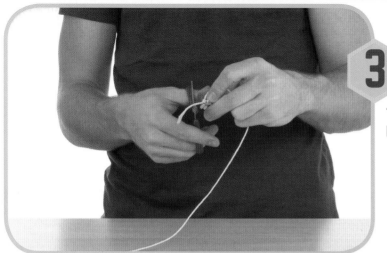

3

TRIM any excess string beyond the knots on either end of the string.

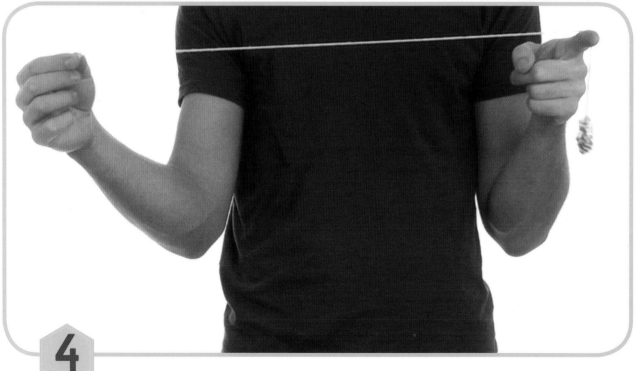

4

GRAB the single-hex nut end of the string with one hand and drape the other, heavier end of the string over your opposite hand's pointing index finger. Pull the single-hex nut end of the string so that the 14 hex nuts are touching your pointing index finger. Make sure that the string is parallel or close to parallel with the ground.

PENDULUM CATCH

READ (AND THINK THROUGH) THIS NEXT PART BEFORE YOU DO IT:

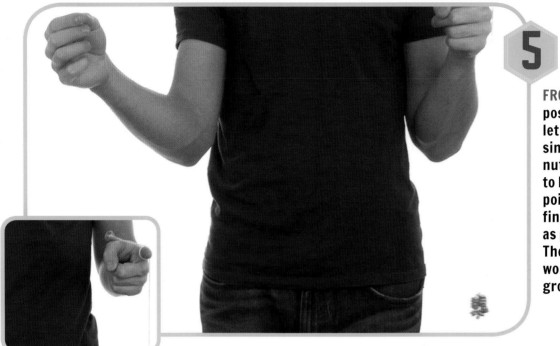

5

FROM this position, let go of the single hex nut. Be sure to keep your pointing index finger as still as possible. The hex nuts won't hit the ground!

HOW DOES IT WORK?

A pendulum is a weight suspended from a pivot (or fixed point) so that it can swing freely, back and forth. Pendulums like this one operate using acceleration from gravity, and the ideal ratio of weight between the two objects at either end of the string should be about 14-to-1, hence the 15 hex nuts. When you release the single hex nut, gravity accelerates it toward the ground, giving it velocity.

In a normal pendulum, the velocity and amplitude (how high the pendulum swings) decrease as the pendulum swings. In our pendulum, the distance between the pivot (your finger) and the bob (the single hex nut) is decreased rapidly when you release the string. As this distance decreases, the velocity of the pendulum increases, and its amplitude is increased to a point that it makes several full swings, wrapping the string around your finger. Friction keeps the group of hex nuts from falling to the ground. With each turn around your finger, the friction increases and stops the fall of the stack of hex nuts.

The dangling object appears to defy gravity thanks to kinetic (or moving) energy and potential (or stored) energy. When you hold the pendulum apparatus in your fingers, both ends of the string have potential energy. Once you let go of the single hex nut, its potential energy turns into kinetic energy as it drops. The falling hex nut builds up speed, or increases its kinetic energy, causing the end of the string to wrap itself around your finger.

TAKE IT FURTHER

Experiment with changing the incline angle of the string—when the string is at a much sharper angle, does the same thing happen as when the string is horizontally parallel to the ground? How many (or how few) hex nuts can you add to the lighter side of the pendulum and still have it work?

KINETIC ENERGY DESCRIBES THE ENERGY OF A MOVING OBJECT.

POTENTIAL ENERGY DESCRIBES THE STORED ENERGY IN A STATIONARY OBJECT.

Did you know?

IN 1851, FRENCH PHYSICIST LÉON FOUCAULT CREATED A PENDULUM TO DEMONSTRATE THE EARTH'S ROTATION BY SUSPENDING A LEAD BOB FROM THE DOME OF THE PANTHÉON IN PARIS. TODAY, FOUCAULT PENDULUMS CAN BE FOUND AROUND THE WORLD.

BURPING BOTTLE

GLASS OBJECTS CAN'T BURP, RIGHT?

MATERIALS

 Dime

Glass Bottle

Straw

Cup of Water

LET'S EXPERIMENT

1 PLACE a dime over the mouth of a glass bottle.

2 CAREFULLY put the bottle (with the dime covering the mouth) in a freezer for several hours. The colder the bottle is, the better.

3 REMOVE the bottle from the freezer.

4 DIP one end of a straw into a cup of water. Press your thumb tightly to the other end of the straw to lift a small amount of water out of the cup. (Don't let go yet!)

5 POSITION the water-filled straw over the dime. Remove your thumb from the end of the straw, allowing the water to pour onto the dime.

SIT BACK and observe! The dime is lifted off of the mouth of the bottle by a burp from inside the bottle.

HOW DOES IT WORK?

Placing the dime over the mouth of the bottle creates a seal that traps air inside the bottle. As the bottle chills in the freezer, these air particles begin to slow down and become more dense due to low air pressure. Removing the bottle from the freezer exposes the trapped cold air to a much warmer climate—the air quickly expands, raising the pressure inside the bottle.

Dropping water on top of the dime creates a slightly better seal than the dime alone thanks to the hydrogen bonds between molecules of water. These hydrogen bonds create cohesion (the act of the water molecules clinging to each other) and adhesion (the act of the water molecules clinging to the mouth of the bottle). The water allows you to see the expanding air trying to escape through the mouth of the bottle. This increased air pressure pushes against the watery seal and lifts the dime just slightly. When hydrogen bonds break—burp!—the dime returns to its flat position.

Did you know?

DIMES ARE THE SMALLEST AND THINNEST U.S. COINS IN USE TODAY. THE WORD DIME COMES FROM THE FRENCH WORD DISME, PRONOUNCED "DEEM," WHICH WAS BASED ON THE LATIN WORD DECIMUS, MEANING "ONE TENTH."

QUICK-POUR SODA BOTTLE RACE

LET'S EXPERIMENT

THE SECRET'S IN THE SWIRL!

MATERIALS

2 1-Liter Plastic Soda Bottles

Pitcher of Water

Large Bowl

Washer

Duct Tape

Stopwatch or Watch with a Second Hand

1

REMOVE the label from the soda bottles so you have a clear view of the inside. Fill one soda bottle almost to the top with water.

2

Have a friend or an adult help you with this step: PLACE your hand over the opening of the bottle. Without squeezing the sides, turn the bottle upside down over the large bowl. Remove your hand and time how long it takes to empty all of the water. Repeat this several times and average the results. Call this the Glug-Glug Method.

3

REFILL the bottle almost to the top with the same amount of water as you did before and replace your hand on top. This time, after you turn it over, move or swirl the bottle in a tight, clockwise or counterclockwise circular motion until you see what looks like a tornado in the bottle—a vortex. Remove your hand and the water flows out quickly. Time it and call it the Vortex Method. Repeat the test several times and average the results for each method. Which one allows the water to exit the bottle more quickly?

4

REFILL the bottle and put a washer on the lip of the bottle.

QUICK-POUR SODA BOTTLE RACE

5

TEAR Tear off a piece of duct tape and use it to secure the mouth of the second (empty) bottle to the mouth of the first bottle with the washer sandwiched in between.

6

TURN the entire contraption upside down and swirl until a tornado forms, driving the water down into the second bottle. As you can see, this dual bottle construct enables you to test different vortex speeds without having to refill the bottle after each attempt!

HOW DOES IT WORK?

This vortex is created when a rotating liquid falls through an opening. Gravity pulls the liquid into the hole, and the rotation causes a continuous vortex to develop.

   Swirling the water is key to creating the vortex, which makes it easier for air to come into the bottle and allows the water to pour out quickly. If you do not swirl the water but just allow it to flow out on its own, the air and the water have to take turns passing through the mouth of the bottle (hence the glug-glug sound).

TAKE IT FURTHER

See if you can figure out new methods for getting the water out quickly. Time your trials and record them, or take science into your own hands and challenge your friends to a race!

A VORTEX IS A TYPE OF MOTION THAT CAUSES LIQUIDS AND GASES TO TRAVEL IN SPIRALS AROUND A CENTERLINE.

Did you know?

A TORNADO THAT FORMS OVER A BODY OF WATER IS CALLED A WATERSPOUT.

43

AIR PRESSURE CAN CRUSHER

WATCH A CAN IMPLODE BEFORE YOUR EYES!

MATERIALS

Safety Goggles

Hot Plate or Electric Stove Top

Gloves

Tongs

Empty Clean Soda Cans

Water

Bowl

LET'S EXPERIMENT

1 RINSE OUT the soda cans to remove any leftover soda goo. Fill the bowl with cold water (the colder, the better).

2

ADD 1 generous tablespoon of water to the empty soda can to cover the bottom of the can.

3

PLACE the can directly on the hot plate (or electric burner) while it is in the "OFF" position, then ask an adult to turn on the burner to heat the water. Once you see the water vapor rising out of the can, continue heating the can for one more minute.

AIR PRESSURE CAN CRUSHER

READ (AND THINK THROUGH) THIS NEXT PART BEFORE YOU DO IT:

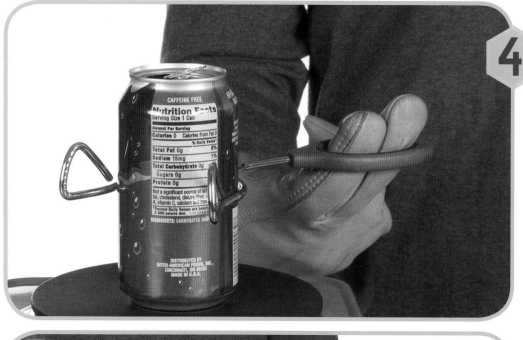

4

HOLD the tongs so that your hand is in the palm up position and grab the can.

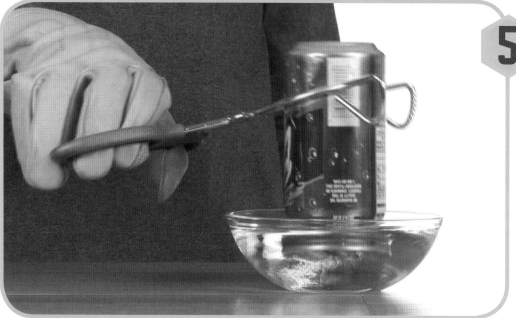

5

IN ONE swift motion, lift the can off the burner, turn it upside down and plunge it into the water.

6

WATCH as the can implodes! Repeat the experiment with the other cans.

HOW DOES IT WORK?

Before heating, the can is filled with water and air. By boiling the water, the water changes states from a liquid to a gas called water vapor, which pushes the air that was originally inside the can out into the atmosphere. When the can is turned upside down and placed in the bowl, the mouth of the can forms an airtight seal against the surface of the water. In a split second, all of the water vapor inside of the can turns into only a drop or two of liquid, which takes up much less space. This small amount of water cannot exert much pressure on the inside walls of the can. The result: the pressure of the air outside of the can is far greater than the pressure inside it. This drastic difference in pressure completely crushes the can—an effect scientists call an implosion.

You also may have noticed the can was filled with water after it imploded. This is a great illustration of how air is pushing all around us. In this case, the outside air pressure was pushing downward on the surface of the water in the bowl. Since the air pressure inside the can was less than the pressure outside the can, water from the bowl was literally pushed up and into the can as it collapsed.

Did you know?

ORIGINALLY PACKAGED IN TIN-PLATED STEEL, CANNED BEVERAGES FIRST HIT THE MARKET IN THE LATE 1930S. BUT DESIGN PROBLEMS AND METAL SHORTAGES DURING WORLD WAR II FORCED SOFT DRINK COMPANIES TO GET CREATIVE, AND BY THE 1960S, RECYCLABLE ALUMINUM SODA CANS AS WE KNOW THEM TODAY BECAME THE NORM.

WATER BALLOON IN A BOTTLE

LET'S EXPERIMENT

AIR PRESSURE IS THE KEY TO THIS "IMPOSSIBLE" TRICK.

MATERIALS

- 1-Liter Bottle
- Water
- Duct Tape
- Balloon
- Tack or Pushpin

1

INSERT the bulb of the balloon into the bottle. Wrap the open end of the balloon around the mouth of the bottle.

2

TAKE a deep breath and try to blow up the balloon. No matter how hard you try, it doesn't blow up!

3

USE the tack or pushpin to poke a tiny hole in the bottom of the bottle.

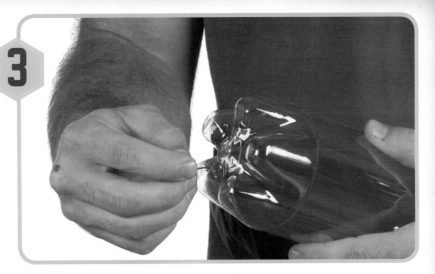

4

TAKE another deep breath and try blowing up the balloon. Success!

WHILE the balloon is still inflated, cover the hole in the bottom of the bottle with a finger and take your mouth off of the balloon. It stays inflated!

5

WATER BALLOON IN A BOTTLE

6 **TAKE** your finger off of the hole, and the balloon deflates.

TO MAKE the water balloon: Blow up the balloon as directed in Steps 4 and 5, then cover the hole in the bottle with a piece of duct tape so that the balloon stays inflated. Make sure you secure it well enough that the tape will be able to hold for a while.

7

8

FILL the inflated balloon with water and tie off the balloon. You've achieved the water balloon in a bottle!

HOW DOES IT WORK?

Although the bottle appears empty, it's actually filled with air. Before you poke a hole in the bottle, the only way for the air to escape is through the mouth of the bottle. Once the mouth is covered with the balloon, the air is trapped inside. When you try to blow up the balloon, it won't inflate much the first time due to the air filling the bottle because there's no room for it to expand.

But when you punch a hole in the bottle, the air molecules in the bottle have an exit, and they're pushed out as the balloon fills the space. As long as you plug the hole, the balloon stays inflated because there is no air rushing back in to push on it. When you take your finger off the hole, air flows back in and pushes the air (or water) inside of the balloon back out of the bottle. Due to the elasticity of the rubber or latex, the balloon shrinks to its original size as this happens.

TAKE IT FURTHER

Suppose your finger gets tired while the balloon is inflated. Put a cap tightly on the bottle and remove your finger. For the air to flow, both holes have to be open.

Did you know?

WATER BALLOONS WERE CREATED IN 1950 WHEN ENGLISH INVENTOR EDGAR ELLINGTON FAILED TO CREATE A WATERPROOF SOCK TO PREVENT TRENCH FOOT. AFTER ACCIDENTALLY DAMAGING HIS LATEX CREATION AND DISCOVERING IT WAS NO LONGER WATERPROOF, HE ANGRILY TOSSED IT ONTO A TABLE. WATCHING IT BURST, ELLINGTON SOON CAME UP WITH A SECOND IDEA, WHICH HE THEN CALLED "WATER GRENADES," THE PRECURSOR TO THE WATER BALLOONS OF TODAY.

BLUBBER GLOVE

THIS INSULATED MITT KEEPS YOUR HAND WARM IN ICE WATER!

MATERIALS

- 2 Large Zipper-Lock Bags
- Shortening
- Large Spoon
- Duct Tape
- Water
- Ice
- Bucket

LET'S EXPERIMENT

1 FILL half of a one- or two-gallon bucket with cold water, then add lots of ice.

2 FILL a zipper-lock bag with three or four heaping spoonfuls of shortening.

3

PUT your hand inside a second zipper-lock bag of the same size as the first and push it into the shortening-filled zipper-lock bag.

4

SPREAD the shortening around the zipper-lock bags until the inner bag is mostly covered.

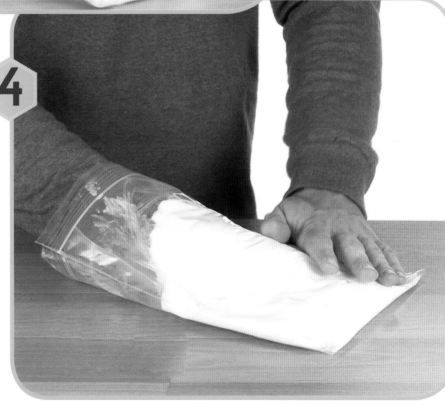

BLUBBER GLOVE

5

FOLD the top of the inner zipper-lock bag over the top of the outer zipper-lock bag, keeping the shortening between the two. Duct tape the fold in place so that the shortening does not come out of the bag.

6

STICK your hand in the glove and dip your blubber-gloved hand into the icy water to put your creation to the test.

Try using other materials following the same steps as before to find out which insulator you think works best:

- Butter
- Margarine
- Cotton Balls
- Starch Peanuts
- Dirt or Sand

HOW DOES IT WORK?

Just like blubber, shortening is a fat, which means it's great for thermoregulation, or keeping the heat in and the cold out. Fats work well as insulators due to their high density and low thermal conductivity relative to water. Despite being submerged in incredibly cold water, fats can maintain a constant temperature. Blubber requires very little blood supply, allowing more blood to be circulated to an animal's skin surfaces that are directly exposed to frigid temperatures. With your hand safely nestled inside the Blubber Glove, the fat takes the full brunt of the cold, just as blubber insulates animals in Arctic and Antarctic waters.

Did you know?

ANCIENT PEOPLES OF THE ARCTIC, LIKE THE ESKIMO AND INUIT OF ALASKA AND CANADA, TRADITIONALLY CONSUMED BLUBBER AS A STAPLE OF THEIR DIETS. WHALE BLUBBER IN PARTICULAR IS AN EXCELLENT SOURCE OF VITAMINS C AND D, WHICH COMES IN HANDY WHEN YOU LIVE IN A REGION WHERE THERE ARE NO CITRUS TREES.

WORLD'S SIMPLEST MOTOR

MAKE AN ELECTRIC MOTOR IN MINUTES!

MATERIALS

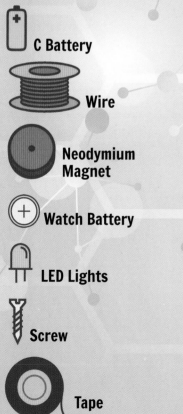

- C Battery
- Wire
- Neodymium Magnet
- Watch Battery
- LED Lights
- Screw
- Tape

LET'S EXPERIMENT

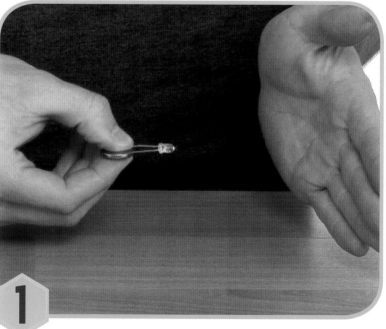

1

POSITION the watch battery between the two legs of an LED light. Make sure the longer leg is on the positive (+) side, or "pole," of the battery. Pinch the legs to the battery and the LED will start to glow.

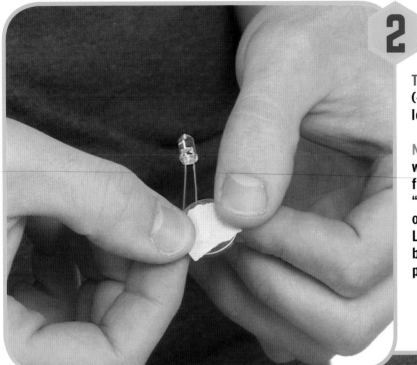

2

TAPE the shorter leg to the negative (-) side of the battery. Don't tape the longer leg.

NOTE: When a device functions only with a certain direction of electron flow (like an LED), it's said to be a "polar sensitive" device (because of the "poles" on a battery). The LED won't work if you reverse the battery. Try it! The longer leg is the positive side of the LED.

3

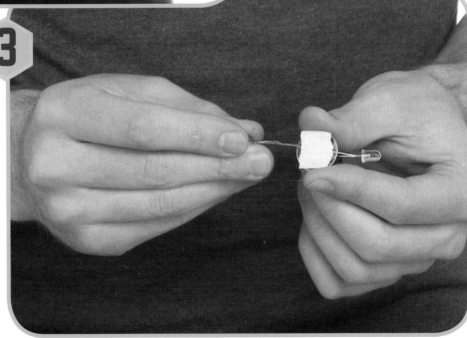

SLIDE the shorter leg of the second LED under the tape on the negative pole of the battery. The LEDs should be 180° apart from each other to balance the battery. Do a "sanity check" and pinch the four legs to the battery to make sure both LEDs are working.

WORLD'S SIMPLEST MOTOR

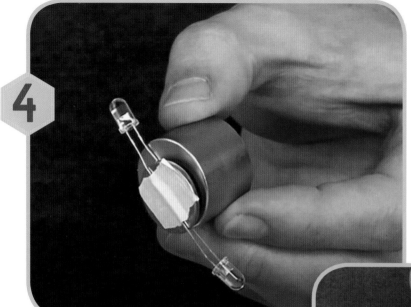

4

ATTACH the positive pole of the battery to one end of the magnet. Center the battery as much as possible so the LEDs are balanced—they should now be glowing.

NOTE: Neodymium magnets are strong, so watch out for pinched fingers.

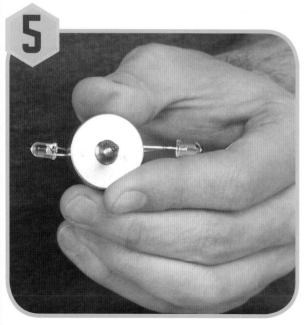

5

CENTER the flat screw head on the other end of the magnet.

6

PLACE the tip of the screw in the center of the negative (flat) end of the C battery.

7

BEND the wire to touch one end to the positive (raised) end of the C battery and the other end of the wire to the magnet. When the spinning starts, remove the wire.

HOW DOES IT WORK?

In this simple electric motor, the wire connects the positive battery terminal to the negative terminal through the magnet and the screw, forming a complete circuit, which means a current of electrons flows in the wire. The presence of the magnet, however, changes things: The current actually flows within a magnetic field. When a current flows in a magnetic field, it experiences something called the Lorentz force. This force is applied perpendicular to both the current's direction and the direction of the magnetic field. The Lorentz force is exerted on charged particles (electrons or protons) moving with a velocity (with speed and direction) through electric and magnetic fields at the same time. But the Lorentz force is present only when the current flows. As soon as the wire is removed, it stops. The magnet acts like a fly wheel and continues to spin because friction between the positive pole of the battery and the tip of the screw is so low. The LEDs display this movement in a dramatic (and really cool!) way.

Did you know?

ALSO KNOWN AS A HOMOPOLAR MOTOR FOR ITS DUAL MAGNETIC POLES, THIS DEVICE WAS FIRST INVENTED IN 1821 BY ENGLISH SCIENTIST MICHAEL FARADAY, ONLY 21 YEARS AFTER THE FIRST ELECTRIC BATTERY WAS CREATED.

AMAZING 9-LAYER DENSITY TOWER

DOUBLE DOWN ON DENSITY!

MATERIALS

- Large Glass Vase
- Honey
- Corn Syrup
- 100% Maple Syrup
- Whole Milk
- Dish Soap
- Water
- Vegetable Oil
- Rubbing Alcohol
- Lamp Oil
- 9 Cups
- Turkey Baster
- Food Coloring
- Bolt
- Popcorn Kernel
- Die
- Cherry Tomato
- Beads
- Soda Bottle Cap
- Ping-Pong ball

1 POUR equal amounts of each liquid in the cups. Set the cups in the order you'll add them into the container: honey, corn syrup, maple syrup, whole milk, dish soap, water, vegetable oil, rubbing alcohol and lamp oil. You can add food coloring to the water and the rubbing alcohol for contrast so they stand out in the finished column.

2 POUR the honey into the cylinder. (NOTE: It's very important to slowly layer the honey, corn syrup and maple syrup into the center of the cylinder. Take your time and make sure they don't touch the sides of the cylinder as you pour.)

3 POUR the corn syrup into the cylinder, followed by the maple syrup.

4 USE the turkey baster to slowly and carefully layer the milk, followed by the dish soap, a little at a time.

5 STARTING with the water, hold the tip of the baster against the side of the container close to the layer of dish soap. Squeeze gently and slowly so the water flows down the side of the container and onto the dish soap. Move the baster upward as needed.

AMAZING 9-LAYER DENSITY TOWER

LAYER the vegetable oil, the rubbing alcohol and the lamp oil in the same way. Allow the layers to settle and separate.

7

RELEASE the objects one at a time into the tower (starting with the bolt, then the popcorn kernel, game die, cherry tomato, plastic beads, soda bottle cap and the ping-pong ball) so they "slide" as gently as possible through the liquids and fall along the side of the container. Release them at different spots around the container to avoid causing too much turbulence in the same location. Allow the upper layers to settle completely between each release.

OBSERVE and pay close attention. What do you notice about the liquids as you add them into the tower? Take note of each object as you release. How far does each one travel through the liquids? Why do you think that is?

HOW DOES IT WORK?

Density is basically how much "stuff" is packed into a particular volume, or a comparison between an object's mass and its volume. Remember: density = mass ÷ volume. If the weight (or mass) of something increases but the volume stays the same, then density goes up. Likewise, if the mass decreases but the volume stays the same, then density goes down. Lighter liquids (such as water or vegetable oil) are less dense than heavier liquids (such as honey or corn syrup), so they float on top of the heavier liquids, whereas the liquids that weigh more (a higher density) will sink below the liquids that weigh less (a lower density). As for the objects, the metal bolt sinks directly to the bottom because it is the most dense. Less dense objects, like the beads, will float on individual liquid layers up the column, leaving the ping-pong ball, the least dense of all, to float on top.

TAKE IT FURTHER

Try using a kitchen scale to weigh an equal volume of each liquid. Does the honey weigh more than the dish soap? Which liquids are lighter than water?

Did you know?

DUE TO THEIR BUOYANCY, PING-PONG BALLS WERE ONCE PROPOSED AS A MEANS TO RAISE THE WRECK OF THE *TITANIC*, BUT THE IMPRACTICAL PLAN NEVER MATERIALIZED. SURPRISINGLY, A 2004 EPISODE OF *MYTHBUSTERS* PROVED FILLING A MUCH SMALLER SUNKEN VESSEL WITH PING-PONG BALLS TO BRING IT TO THE WATER'S SURFACE COULD ACTUALLY WORK!

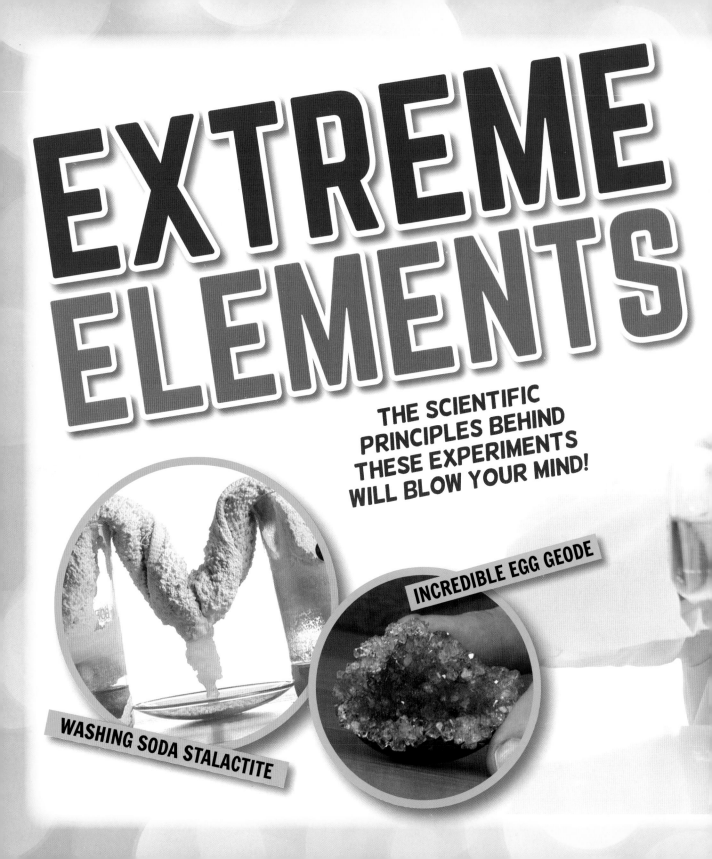

EXTREME ELEMENTS

THE SCIENTIFIC
PRINCIPLES BEHIND
THESE EXPERIMENTS
WILL BLOW YOUR MIND!

INCREDIBLE EGG GEODE

WASHING SODA STALACTITE

BUILD A LIGHT BULB

See page 76 to learn how pencil lead can light up a room!

COLORFUL COINS

THERE'S MORE TO THIS DYE THAN MEETS THE EYE.

MATERIALS

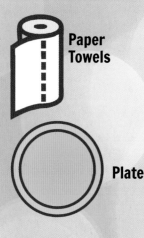

Paper Towels

Plate

Distilled White Vinegar

Dime

Nickel

NOTE: THIS EXPERIMENT REQUIRES 24 HOURS

LET'S EXPERIMENT

1

PLACE two sheets of paper towels on a plate. Pour a small amount of vinegar in the center of the paper towels.

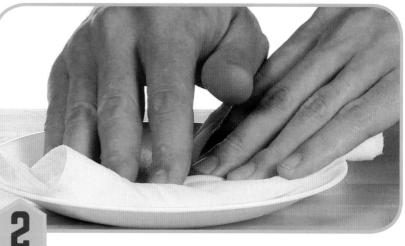

2

PLACE the coins in the center of the plate. Fold over the sides of the paper towels to cover the coins completely.

3

SOAK the entire paper towel with vinegar, allowing the coins to sit (and soak) for about 24 hours.

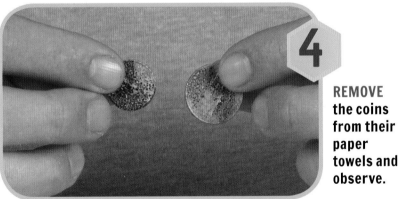

4

REMOVE the coins from their paper towels and observe.

HOW DOES IT WORK?

Nickels and dimes are made of nickel and copper. You may have heard vinegar makes a great cleaning agent for copper, and that's true. But if vinegar is allowed to stay on copper, it will slowly turn the surface bluish-green, a distinct sign of verdigris. A common sign of corrosion, verdigris can be copper carbonate, copper chloride or copper acetate. All of these compounds appear as a bluish-green coating. In this experiment, it can take almost a whole day for the compounds to begin accumulating on the surface of your coins.

Did you know?

IF YOU'VE SEEN THE STATUE OF LIBERTY, YOU'VE SEEN VERDIGRIS IN ACTION! THE STATUE WAS INITIALLY A SHINY COPPER COLOR WHEN IT WAS INSTALLED ON LIBERTY ISLAND IN 1886. BUT LIKE OTHER BRONZE, COPPER OR BRASS OBJECTS LEFT TO OXIDIZE IN THE ELEMENTS, THE MONUMENT TURNED BLUISH-GREEN OVER THE YEARS, TAKING ON ITS CURRENT HUE AROUND 1920.

WASHING SODA STALACTITE

SPEED UP GEOLOGY WITH A CAVE PILLAR THAT FORMS IN DAYS, NOT CENTURIES!

MATERIALS

- Washing Soda
- Hot Water
- Small Plate
- Washcloth
- String
- 2 Beakers (or Tall Glasses)
- Scissors
- Spoon

NOTE: THIS EXPERIMENT REQUIRES 3-5 DAYS

LET'S EXPERIMENT

1 FILL two beakers with hot water. Leave about an inch at the top of each beaker to avoid spilling the water during the rest of the experiment.

2 ADD approximately ½ cup of washing soda to each beaker and stir both beakers until all of the washing soda is dissolved.

3

FOLD the washcloth in half diagonally, making a triangle. Roll it up tightly.

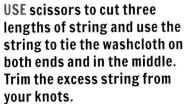

USE scissors to cut three lengths of string and use the string to tie the washcloth on both ends and in the middle. Trim the excess string from your knots.

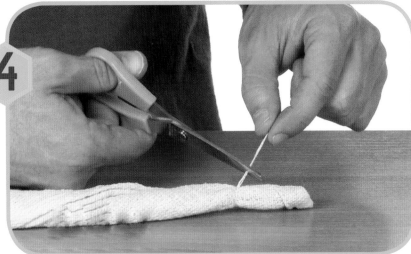

4

5

PLACE each end of the washcloth in its own beaker. Make sure the ends touch the bottoms of the beakers.

WASHING SODA STALACTITE

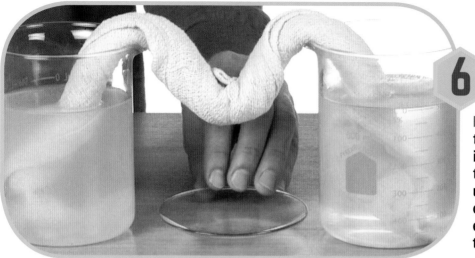

6

PULL the center of the rag down so that it dips toward the table. Put the plate under the center of the rag. Let your experiment sit for three to five days.

7

CHECK BACK during the waiting period to see the progress and watch the stalactite form. After the waiting period is up, you should have a pillar that stretches all the way from the washcloth to the plate!

HOW DOES IT WORK?

Remember how you added the washing soda to the beakers by stirring it into hot water? Hot water is more accepting of additives like washing soda, so you can mix more washing soda into hot water than you can into cold water.

To kick off the stalactite formation, the washcloth has to transfer the water and dissolved washing soda from the beakers to the plate. This principle is called capillary action, the same process that enables plants and trees to transfer water and nutrients from the ground up through their roots and trunks and into their leaves, branches, flowers and fruit. The washcloth uses capillary action to soak itself in the washing soda solution until it's too saturated to hold any more liquid. Once the washcloth is over-saturated, the excess washing soda solution begins to drip from the lowest part of the washcloth right over the plate.

As the water cools and drips from the washcloth, small amounts of the washing soda are deposited onto the plate below. Eventually, the excess washing soda forms a complete pillar.

TAKE IT FURTHER

Try testing different dissolvable substances such as salt or baking soda. Which substance creates the largest pillar? Which substance creates a pillar the quickest? Try altering the heights of the beakers and dip in the center of the washcloth. How does this change the shape or size of the pillar?

Did you know?

STALACTITES TAKE THOUSANDS OF YEARS TO FORM AS PRECIPITATION DRIPS DOWN THROUGH A CAVE'S CEILING. LIMESTONE STALACTITES FORM FROM CALCITE MINERALS, BUT CAN FEATURE GYPSUM, ARAGONITE OR OTHER INCLUSIONS. ROCK FORMATIONS THAT RISE FROM THE CAVE FLOOR ARE CALLED STALAGMITES.

INCREDIBLE EGG GEODE

GROW YOUR OWN CRYSTALLIZED WONDER!

🕐 **NOTE: THIS EXPERIMENT REQUIRES 2-3 DAYS**

MATERIALS

- Egg
- Small Paintbrush
- Glue
- Food Coloring
- Water
- Alum Powder
- Scissors
- Paper Towels
- Bowl
- Beaker
- Tack or Pushpin
- Spoon

LET'S EXPERIMENT

1 CAREFULLY wash each egg before you put your mouth on it (see below). Use the pushpin to make a hole in each end of the egg.

2 WHILE holding the egg over the bowl, put your mouth on one end and blow the yolk and the egg white through the other hole. This may take a while, so don't rush.

3

INSERT one scissor blade into one of the holes in the egg, then slowly and gently cut the shell in half, down the egg's length.

4

CAREFULLY wash the inside of the halved shell (or shells, if you want to make a second geode later) with warm water and use a paper towel to wipe it dry. Get the interior of the egg as clean and dry as possible without cracking it. Peel off and throw away any small pieces of shell around the edge.

5

POUR some glue into the eggshell. Use the paintbrush to completely coat the inside of the shell with glue. Make sure to cover the edges of the shell as well. Use more glue if needed.

6

LAY the glue-coated eggshell open-side-up on a paper towel. Generously sprinkle the alum powder to coat the glue in and on the eggshell.

INCREDIBLE EGG GEODE

CAREFULLY turn the alum-covered eggshell upside-down over the paper towel and gently tap out the excess alum powder. Place it on a fresh paper towel (or on a paper plate) and allow it to dry overnight.

7

8

FILL the beaker with two cups of hot water, almost to a boil. Add 30 drops of food coloring in a color of your choosing to the water and stir well.

9

ADD ¾ cup of alum powder to the beaker and stir until the alum is completely dissolved. Let the mixture cool for 30 minutes.

10

SLOWLY place the shell into the solution alum-side up and use a spoon to gently push it to the bottom. Let it sit for 12 to 15 hours.

11

USE a spoon to transfer the eggshell from the beaker to a paper towel for drying. Wait for the eggshell to dry completely before touching your creation.

HOW DOES IT WORK?

A geode is a mass of minerals within a rock that is formed through a process called sedimentation. In nature, these minerals take thousands or even millions of years to form deep in the earth, but your Incredible Egg Geode takes only a couple of days! The heated alum solution contains suspended particles of alum powder; as the solution cools, these particles gradually fall and settle on the bottom of the beaker, where they begin to crystallize.

Coating the shell with alum powder beforehand gives the alum particles suspended in the water a surface to which they can more readily attach themselves. The particles that settle on the interior of the shell crystallize quickly, but you can also see evidence of crystallization on other parts of the shell as well as on the bottom and sides of the beaker.

Did you know?

ALSO KNOWN AS A "THUNDER EGG," THE GEODE IS THE OFFICIAL STATE ROCK OF IOWA AND OREGON.

BUILD A LIGHT BULB

CREATE A BATTERY-POWERED LIGHT BULB!

MATERIALS

- 8 D Batteries
- Electrical Tape
- .5 mm Pencil Lead
- Scissors
- 2 Wires with Alligator Clips
- Toilet Paper Roll
- Jar
- Pie Plate

LET'S EXPERIMENT

1

CUT seven pieces of electrical tape and use them to fix eight D-sized batteries together, end-to-end, with the positive ends connected to the negative ends.

2

USE scissors to cut a toilet paper tube to a height that will fit comfortably inside a mason jar or other clear glass (be sure to leave plenty of room). This is your stand for the alligator clips.

3

TAPE the wires with the alligator clips opposite one another on the outside of the toilet paper tube. The clips themselves should rest just past the end of the tube.

4

TAPE the tube with the clips to a pie pan (or other heat resistant surface) so that it stands upright, clips pointing upward.

5

CAREFULLY clip a mechanical pencil refill between the two alligator clips. The pencil refill needs to be in one piece, so be gentle.

BUILD A LIGHT BULB

6 PLACE a mason jar or clear glass over the top of the toilet paper tube stand.

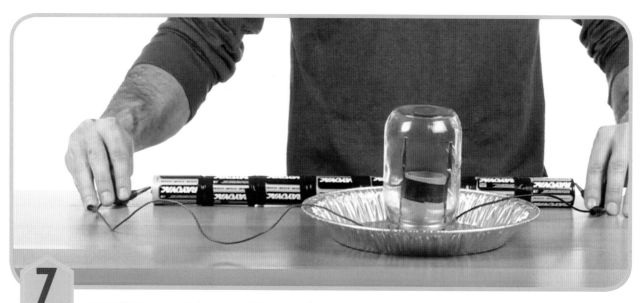

7 TOUCH the remaining two alligator clips at the free ends of the wires to the positive and negative ends of your super battery.

8

GIVE the circuit a moment to circulate the electricity and watch the pencil refill begin to glow.

HOW DOES IT WORK?

When you touch the free ends of the alligator clips to your "super battery," you form a complete circuit, which means electricity flows freely through the entire apparatus you just built. As this flow of electricity channels through the graphite-based mechanical pencil refill, the refill begins to glow and give off smoke and light. This happens because the electricity heats the graphite refill to an incredible temperature.

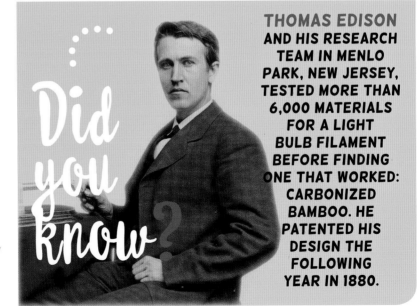

Did you know?

THOMAS EDISON AND HIS RESEARCH TEAM IN MENLO PARK, NEW JERSEY, TESTED MORE THAN 6,000 MATERIALS FOR A LIGHT BULB FILAMENT BEFORE FINDING ONE THAT WORKED: CARBONIZED BAMBOO. HE PATENTED HIS DESIGN THE FOLLOWING YEAR IN 1880.

COLORFUL CONVECTION CURRENTS

LET'S EXPERIMENT

TAKE A CLOSER LOOK AT WEATHER SCIENCE IN A BOTTLE.

MATERIALS

4 Empty Identical Bottles

Water

Food Coloring

Playing Cards

Paper Towels

1

FILL two of the four bottles with cold water. Be sure to fill each bottle to the brim. Add blue food coloring to each of these bottles.

2

FILL the remaining two bottles with hot water from your tap. It should not be so hot that it burns. Add yellow food coloring to these bottles.

3

PLACE a card over the mouth of a (yellow) hot water bottle. Read through this next part before you do it: Holding the card in place, turn the bottle upside down and place it on top of the (blue) cold water bottle. The two bottles should be mouth-to-mouth with the card separating the two liquids. Have paper towels close by in case everything doesn't go exactly as planned.

4 WHILE holding the top bottle steady, carefully slide the card out from between the two bottles.

5 PLACE the second (blue) bottle of cold water on top of the (yellow) hot water bottle. Repeat Steps 3 and 4 and carefully remove the card. Observe.

HOW DOES IT WORK?

Hot air balloons rise because warm air is lighter and less dense than cold air. The same goes for warm water: when the bottle of hot or warm water is placed on top of the bottle of cold water, the less dense warm water is confined to the top and the dense cold water stays in the bottom. But when the cold water bottle is placed on top of the warm water bottle, the less dense warm water rises into the top bottle while the cold water sinks to the bottom. This movement, called a convection current, results in the yellow and blue food colorings mixing to create a green liquid. When warm and cold air masses collide in the atmosphere, these convection currents create thunderstorms.

Did you know?

DUE TO ITS LOCATION AT THE FOOT OF THE ROCKY MOUNTAINS, THE CITY OF DENVER, COLORADO, IS PRONE TO TEMPERATURE INVERSIONS IN WHICH WARM AIR HIGHER IN THE ATMOSPHERE TRAPS THE COOLER MOUNTAIN AIR CLOSER TO THE GROUND. THE WARM AIR BARRIER PREVENTS POLLUTANTS FROM ESCAPING INTO THE ATMOSPHERE AND RESULTS IN A "BROWN CLOUD" OF DIRTY AIR AND SMOGGY SKIES, A PHENOMENON WHICH HAS ALSO PLAGUED CITIES LIKE LONDON, VIENNA, BEIJING AND OTHER LOCATIONS WORLDWIDE.

ERUPTING VOLCANO

NO MAGMA REQUIRED!

MATERIALS

Construction Paper

Tape

Small Glass

Scissors

Hydrogen Peroxide

Quick-Rising Yeast

Metal Spoon

Flat Tray or Pan

Measuring Utensils

LET'S EXPERIMENT

1

CUT a strip of construction paper that measures 8 inches long by 3 inches wide.

2

USING the strip of construction paper, form an open ended cone that is large enough to fit over the small glass. Make sure the smaller opening—the top of the cone—is large enough to fit your metal spoon through. Tape the ends to secure the cone shape. Using the scissors, trim the bottom of the cone so that it sits flat on the tray or pan.

3 MEASURE and pour ½ cup of hydrogen peroxide into the small glass.

4 PLACE the glass in the center of the tray or pan, then place the cone over the glass.

5 MEASURE and pour ½ tablespoon of quick-rising yeast into the bottle, then use the metal spoon to stir quickly. Observe.

HOW DOES IT WORK?

The bubbly foam that shoots out of the glass and down the sides of your paper cone is actually oxygen being rapidly released from the hydrogen peroxide. While hydrogen peroxide will slowly release oxygen molecules on its own, the added yeast acts as a catalyst, speeding up the reaction and giving you a front row seat to your very own tabletop volcanic eruption.

Did you know?

SEVENTY-FIVE PERCENT OF THE EARTH'S VOLCANOES, MORE THAN 450 IN TOTAL, CAN BE FOUND IN AND AROUND THE RING OF FIRE, A NEARLY 25,000-MILE-LONG PATH ALONG THE PACIFIC OCEAN KNOWN FOR HIGH AMOUNTS OF SEISMIC ACTIVITY DUE TO THE FREQUENT MOVEMENT OF TECTONIC PLATES.

CORNSTARCH MONSTERS

SOUND YOU CAN SEE!

MATERIALS

Speaker (the older and bigger, the better)

Cornstarch

Large Mixing Bowl

Plastic Wrap or Garbage Bag

Water

Pitcher

Spoon

Measuring Cup

Gallon-Size Zipper-Lock Bag

LET'S EXPERIMENT

1 MEASURE and pour ¼ cup of cornstarch into the mixing bowl, then slowly add about ½ cup of water. Stir with a spoon or mix with your bare hands. But be warned: it's going to get messy!

CONTINUE adding cornstarch and water in small amounts until you get a mixture that has the consistency of honey. It may take a little work to get this just right.

NOTE: The more cornstarch you add, the more the mixture begins to thicken.

3

TRY rolling the substance into a ball. The moment you stop rolling, it turns back into a dripping liquid! That means it is a non-Newtonian fluid, neither 100 percent solid nor 100 percent liquid. If you try and punch it, it turns solid!

CORNSTARCH MONSTERS

ASK an adult for permission before you do this next part: After first making sure the sound system is off, gently lay the speaker on its back so that the speaker faces upward. Cover the speaker with thin plastic like a trash bag or plastic wrap. Pour the non-Newtonian liquid onto the plastic on top of the speaker cone. Be careful not to overfill!

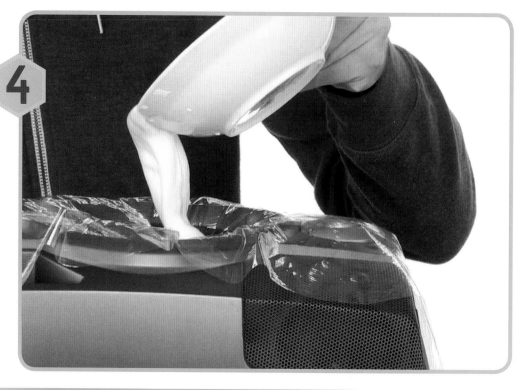

4

5

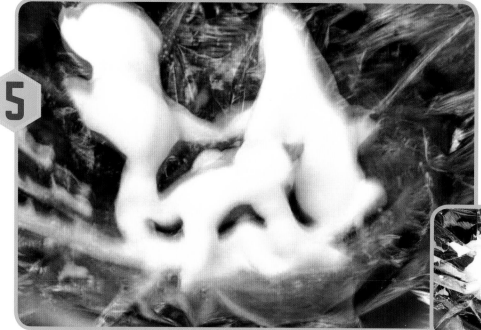

TURN your sound system on and crank up the volume. Pick a song that has a low, consistent bassline, press play and watch what happens to the non-Newtonian liquid. When you turn off the speaker, how does it respond?

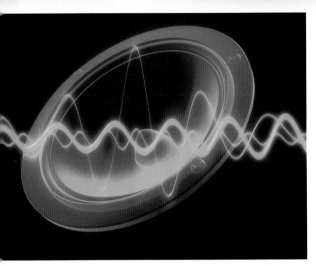

HOW DOES IT WORK?

Lower frequencies—i.e., the sounds of an explosion or a heavy bass line in a song—subject the cornstarch mixture, also called an oobleck, to a lot of movement. Knowledge about sound waves, however, might lead you to think the oobleck would be affected in the exact opposite way. Why? Higher pitched sounds have a higher frequency (meaning there are more vibrations per second). But more vibrations don't equal more movement when it comes to a non-Newtonian fluid. Instead, it's the lower pitched (or lower frequency) sounds which cause the oobleck to shake to the beat. Although there are fewer vibrations per second at lower pitches, these frequencies cause more motion in the speaker cones, helping to move the oobleck along.

To put it in perspective: other non-Newtonian fluids include quicksand, honey and custard. Meanwhile, Newtonian fluids, or fluids which have one constant viscosity, include water, alcohol and gasoline.

TAKE IT FURTHER

What do you think would happen if you tried to run across a small blow-up pool that was filled with oobleck? What if you stood still on top of it?

Did you know?

THE WORD "OOBLECK" COMES FROM THE 1949 DR. SEUSS CLASSIC *BARTHOLOMEW AND THE OOBLECK*, WHICH TELLS THE STORY OF A YOUNG BOY WHO MUST SAVE HIS KINGDOM FROM A MYSTERIOUS GREEN SUBSTANCE THAT FALLS FROM THE SKY.

HOMEMADE MAGNET

MAKE A MAGNET USING ONLY A BATTERY, A NAIL AND SOME WIRE!

⚠️
SAFETY NOTE
Touching a wire to both poles of a battery causes a "short circuit" that quickly drains the battery of its power and can heat up the wire—careful, it could burn your fingers!

MATERIALS

 C Battery

Iron Nail

Insulated Wire with Exposed Ends

 Metal Paper Clips

LET'S EXPERIMENT

1 TOUCH the nail to the paper clips to make sure it's not magnetic.

2

TIGHTLY WRAP the wire around the nail so that it covers about $2/3$ of the nail. You want to make the coils tight and close to each other so there are no gaps between them.

3
PLACE the ends of the wire on the positive and negative ends of the battery.

4
WITH the wire connected to the battery, pass the nail through the paper clips again. Your homemade magnet picks up the paper clips!

TAKE IT FURTHER

What happens if you use different types of batteries to make your electromagnet?

HOW DOES IT WORK?

When an electric current passes through the wire, it creates a magnetic field in the metal core (the nail). When the wire is wrapped around the iron nail and the battery is strong enough, you create a simple electromechanical solenoid, a type of electromagnet. These are typically weak but can be useful over short distances (or for picking up paper clips).

Did you know?

COUNTRIES LIKE CHINA, JAPAN AND SOUTH KOREA HAVE USED ELECTROMAGNETS TO CREATE HIGH-SPEED TRAINS CALLED MAGLEV (MAGNETIC LEVITATION) TRAINS, WHICH FLOAT OVER RAILS AND CAN SAFELY REACH SPEEDS OF UP TO 375 MILES PER HOUR!

ICE-TRAY BATTERY

POWER UP BY COOLING DOWN.

MATERIALS

 Distilled White Vinegar

 5 Pieces of Copper Wire

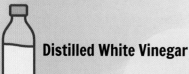 5 Nails

 Ice Tray

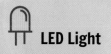 LED Light

LET'S EXPERIMENT

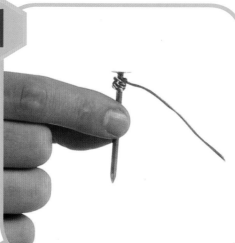

1

TIGHTLY wrap a piece of copper wire five times around a galvanized nail just under the head of the nail. Leave a tail of wire extending straight out from the nail about three inches. Do the same with the remaining four nails and four pieces of copper wire.

2

FILL six wells of an ice tray with distilled white vinegar.

PLACE each wire-wrapped nail into one well of vinegar as shown in the photograph on the right, making sure the copper wire is bent so that it dips into the vinegar in the next well to create a circuit. Make sure the wire from one nail does NOT touch the nail or wire in any other well.

3

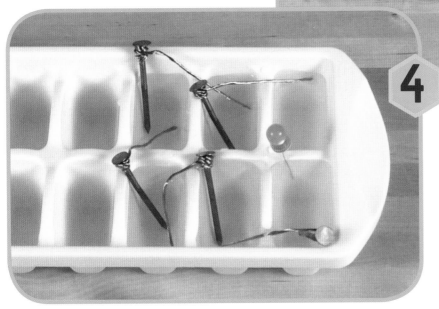

4

PLACE one "leg" of the LED into the last well with the copper wire in it and place the other "leg" into the first well with the nail in it. If the bulb doesn't light up, lift the LED out of the well, rotate it to move the legs to the opposite well, then lower it back into the vinegar. Voilà: It works!

HOW DOES IT WORK?

Remember the Fruit-Power Battery on page 30? In this experiment, you create a battery using vinegar rather than citric acid. The electric current flows from the wire bridge across the vinegar to the nail, along the bridge, then back to the vinegar (and so on). You create a "complete" or closed circuit by connecting the Ice-Tray Battery to the LED. As the electrons pass through the LED, the electrical energy excites the atoms inside it and they emit a specific wavelength of color and allow the LED to glow as they fall back to a lower energy level.

Did you know?

FROM THE FRENCH "VIN AIGRE," OR "SOUR WINE," VINEGAR WAS REPORTEDLY FIRST USED BY THE BABYLONIANS AROUND 3,000 B.C. AS A CONDIMENT AS WELL AS A PICKLING AGENT.

INVISIBLE SODA

WATCH A CHEMICAL REACTION "CLEAR UP" DARK SODA!

MATERIALS

 Milk

Regular Cola

LET'S EXPERIMENT

1 **REMOVE** the label from the bottle so you can fully see the reaction that will soon occur. Slowly open the bottle, then lightly pour in enough milk to raise the level of the cola so it's close to the top.

2 **REPLACE** the bottle cap and screw it on tightly.

3

LET the bottle sit undisturbed in a quiet place for a couple of hours. Keep track of what's going on inside the bottle by taking a photo every 15 minutes or a video.

4

WHEN the time's up, check the bottle: the upper three-quarters of the bottle ends up with a clear liquid in it and the bottom quarter is filled with a solid material.

HOW DOES IT WORK?

When you put drops of vinegar or orange juice into milk, the milk is curdled by the acid content of vinegar (acetic acid) or orange juice (citric acid), and a solid (a precipitate) forms where the drops are. When a cola is diluted with milk, the phosphoric acid in the cola curdles the milk into little globs. The surprising chemical change occurs throughout the bottle, followed by a physical change as the curdled milk slowly falls to the bottom. This chemical change is phosphoric acid in the cola reacting with calcium in the milk to make two new products: tricalcium phosphate and hydrogen. Tricalcium phosphate is the precipitate that falls out of the liquid and settles on the bottom, taking almost all of the caramel coloring in the cola with it. The hydrogen gas bubbles to the top and fills the space under the cap along with the carbon dioxide gas (CO_2) once held in solution by the cola.

Did you know? SOME STUDIES SUGGEST THE HIGH LEVELS OF PHOSPHORIC ACID THAT COME WITH FREQUENT SOFT DRINK CONSUMPTION MIGHT INCREASE THE CHANCE OF OSTEOPOROSIS, WHICH CAUSES CHRONICALLY WEAK, POROUS AND BRITTLE BONES IN THOSE WHO DON'T GET ENOUGH CALCIUM IN THEIR DIET. AN OCCASIONAL SODA POP MAY BE OK, BUT MAKE SURE YOU GET THE CALCIUM YOU NEED EVERY DAY!

NAKED EGG

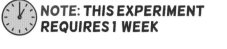

NOTE: **THIS EXPERIMENT REQUIRES 1 WEEK**

WITNESS THE "EGGSHELLENT" DISSOLVING POWER OF VINEGAR.

⚠️ **SAFETY NOTE**
Always wash your hands well with soap and water after handling raw eggs.

MATERIALS

 1 Raw Egg

 Large Glass or Jar

 Distilled White Vinegar

LET'S EXPERIMENT

1

PLACE the egg in a tall glass or jar and cover the egg with vinegar.

2

LOOK CLOSELY at the egg. There will likely be tiny bubbles forming on the shell. Leave the egg in the vinegar for a full 24 hours.

3 CHANGE the vinegar on the second day. Carefully pour the old vinegar down the drain and cover the egg with fresh vinegar. Place the glass with the vinegar and egg in a safe place for seven days, making sure to leave it undisturbed. Pay close attention to the bubbles forming on the surface of the shell (or what's left of it). Over time, you will see the egg lose its shell.

4 AFTER seven days, pour off the vinegar and carefully rinse the egg with water, then gently pat it down with a paper towel. The egg looks translucent because the shell is gone! All that remains is a delicate membrane of the egg surrounding the white and the yolk.

TAKE IT FURTHER

Try using concentrated vinegar instead of traditional vinegar. Concentrated vinegar is about four times the strength of traditional household vinegar. How long does it take the eggshell to dissolve?

HOW DOES IT WORK?

Vinegar is an acid called acetic acid, and white vinegar from the grocery store is usually about 4 percent acetic acid and 96 percent water. Eggshells are made up of calcium carbonate. The acetic acid in the vinegar reacts with the calcium carbonate in the eggshell to make calcium acetate plus water and carbon dioxide (CO_2), which you see as bubbles on the surface of the shell. When the shell is gone, the egg appears translucent. All that remains is the thin membrane called a semipermeable membrane.

And if you'd like to see what happens when you submerge your Naked Egg in a glass of corn syrup or water, see Growing and Shrinking Egg on page 164!

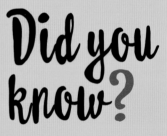

Did you know?

A HEN WILL LAY ABOUT ONE EGG A DAY UNTIL SHE HAS PRODUCED 12 EGGS, CALLED A CLUTCH. SHE WILL THEN SIT ON HER EGGS TO INCUBATE THEM FOR 21 DAYS UNTIL THEY BEGIN TO HATCH.

CO₂ SANDWICH

EXPLORE THE "POP" FACTOR OF VINEGAR AND BAKING SODA.

MATERIALS

Measuring Cup and Spoons

Distilled White Vinegar

Baking Soda

3 Quart-Size Zipper-Lock Bags

3 Snack-Size Zipper-Lock Bags

Safety Glasses

LET'S EXPERIMENT

1 FILL each of the quart-size zipper-lock bags with approximately one tablespoon of baking soda.

2 FILL each of the smaller snack-size zipper-lock bags with varying amounts of vinegar: fill one bag with ¼ cup of vinegar, the next bag with ⅓ cup of vinegar and the last bag with ½ cup of vinegar.

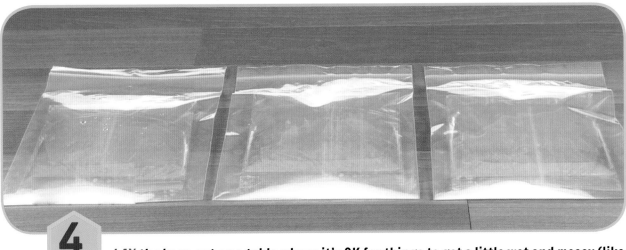

3 SEAL the vinegar bags, leaving as much air inside as possible, then place them inside the larger bags with the baking soda. When you seal the outside bags, however, make sure to remove as much air as possible.

4 LAY the bags out on a table where it's OK for things to get a little wet and messy (like an outdoor table).

CO₂ SANDWICH

5

SMACK your fist down on (or tightly squeeze) the vinegar bags inside the baking soda bags to break them open. The goal is to break open the smaller bag filled with vinegar in order for it to mix with the baking soda. Immediately shake the bags to make sure the substances mix.

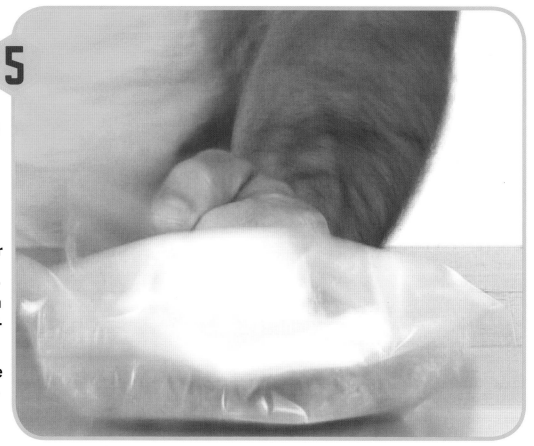

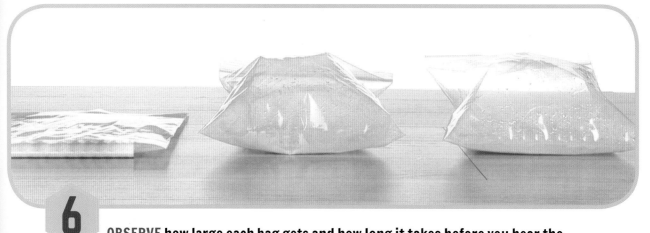

6

OBSERVE how large each bag gets and how long it takes before you hear the giant POP!

TAKE IT FURTHER

Here's a cool twist on the experiment:
Pour four tablespoons of vinegar into a clean empty bottle. Carefully drop one tablespoon of baking soda into the neck of a latex balloon. Shake the balloon to make sure the baking soda falls all the way into the tip of the balloon. Stretch the neck of the balloon over the top of the bottle and gently lift the balloon, making sure that the baking soda drops down into the bottle. As the baking soda reacts with the vinegar, the balloon inflates on its own.

HOW DOES IT WORK?

When you mix vinegar and baking soda, a chemical reaction takes place that produces a gas called carbon dioxide (CO_2). The chemical reaction between the acetic acid in vinegar and the sodium bicarbonate in baking soda results in the formation of sodium acetate, water and carbon dioxide.

The CO_2 takes up lots of space, gradually filling the bag and causing it to puff up. If there's more gas than the bag can hold... BOOM! If you're lucky, the zipper-lock seal will bust open, but the bag will not break. You can reuse the bag to make another CO_2 sandwich. Separating the substances in bags is a clever way of slowing down the reaction.

Did you know?

CARBON DIOXIDE IS USED IN FIRE EXTINGUISHERS AS WELL AS LIFE RAFTS AND LIFE JACKETS, AND IT PROMOTES PLANT GROWTH IN GREENHOUSES. IT EVEN PROVIDES THE FIZZ IN CARBONATED BEVERAGES! FROZEN CARBON DIOXIDE IS CALLED DRY ICE.

VOLCANO IN A CUP

SIMULATE AN UNDERWATER VOLCANO!

MATERIALS

 Electric Burner or Hot Plate

 Heat-Proof Glass Beaker (or Pyrex Measuring Cup)

 Sand

 Wax

Water

LET'S EXPERIMENT

1

PLACE a small piece of wax (about 1-inch by 1-inch) in the bottom of a glass beaker. Pour enough sand into the beaker to completely cover the cube of wax.

2

SLOWLY POUR water into the beaker until it is nearly full (but don't fill it up all the way or you might have some spillage).

3

PLACE the beaker or cup onto a burner or hot plate and set the heat to medium-high.

4 OBSERVE. As the wax heats beneath the sand, it melts and finds its way out of the sandy trap, hardening once again as it cools.

HOW DOES IT WORK?

The core of the earth has liquid hot magma that, on occasion, erupts through the crust. The volcanic eruptions we generally think of occur on land and result in the sky-high smoke plumes and lava flows that we see on the news (which you can replicate by doing the Erupting Volcano experiment on page 82). However, nearly 80 percent of all volcanic eruptions occur underwater. Until scientists got footage of an underwater eruption in 2009, we had no idea what they looked like.

In this experiment, you recreate liquid hot magma by heating wax that is covered by sand. As the liquid hot wax bubbles through the sand, it causes miniature eruptions in the surface of the sand. Think of each bubble in the sand's surface as an underwater volcano. When the wax bubbles through the surface of the sand, it is met by much colder water that cools the wax and causes it to harden.

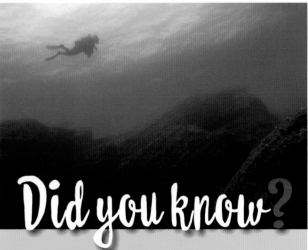

Did you know?

LOCATED UNDER THE PACIFIC OCEAN, TAMU MASSIF, THE WORLD'S LARGEST UNDERWATER VOLCANO, MEASURES ABOUT 100,000 SQUARE MILES. THAT'S ALMOST THE SIZE OF NEW MEXICO!

FUNDAMENTAL FORCES

AFTER THESE EXPERIMENTS, YOU'LL NEVER LOOK AT PHYSICS THE SAME WAY AGAIN!

EGG IN A BOTTLE

ANTI-GRAVITY WATER

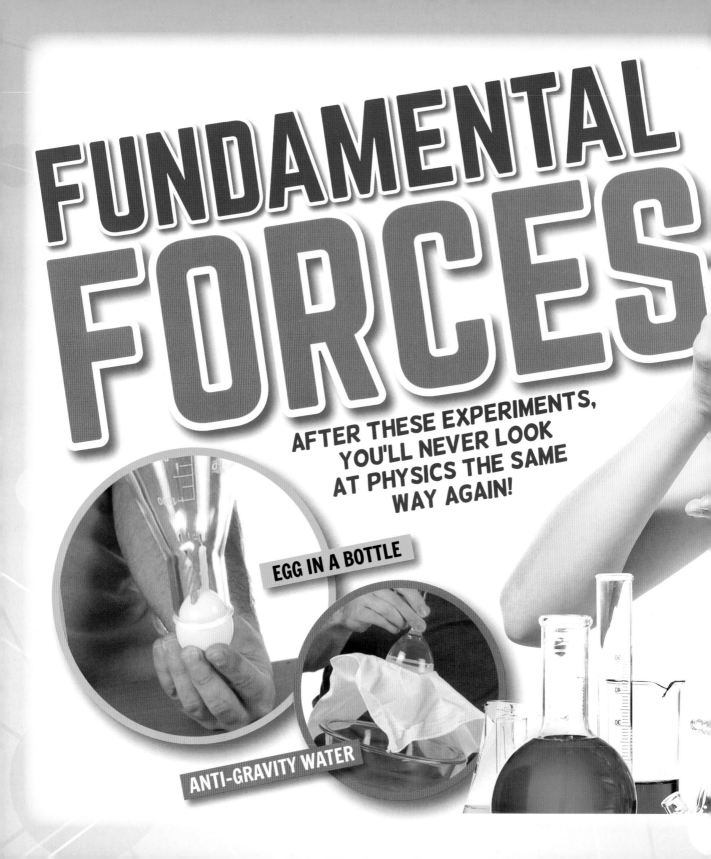

BOUNCING BUBBLE

See page 126 to learn how to make a super strong bubble you can hold!

WATER WHISTLE

TURN A STRAW INTO A MUSICAL INSTRUMENT!

MATERIALS

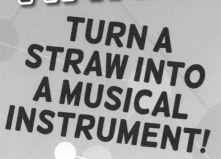

Drinking Straw

Scissors

Glass

Water

LET'S EXPERIMENT

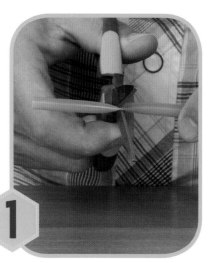

1 CAREFULLY make a PARTIAL cut through the straw a few inches from one end. (Don't snip it off!)

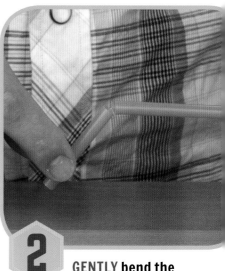

2 GENTLY bend the straw into a right angle at the cut. Be careful not to break the straw in two.

3 FILL ¾ of a cup or glass with water, then slide the bottom of the longer section of straw into the water.

4

KEEP the bent straw at a 90 degree angle. Place your lips on the shorter end of the straw and blow for a few seconds with a light, steady breath. (If you have trouble producing a whistling sound, try pinching the top of the long end of the straw.)

TAKE IT FURTHER

Try raising or lowering the straw to change the pitch.

HOW DOES IT WORK?

All sounds are actually sound waves, vibrations traveling through the air that reach your ears. The longer segment of straw (the one partially submerged in water) contains both air and water. Blowing air across the top of the longer straw segment causes the column of air to vibrate, which creates the whistling sound you hear. Depending on the depth of the straw, the more air that is inside the straw, the lower the pitch of the whistle, while less air will result in a higher pitch.

Did you know?

IN 2018, AS PART OF AN EFFORT TO CUT DOWN ON SINGLE-USE PLASTICS, SEATTLE BECAME THE FIRST U.S. CITY TO ENACT A BAN ON PLASTIC STRAWS.

LED DARTS

GET WIRED WITH CURRENTS AND CIRCUITS.

⚠️

SAFETY NOTE

Neodymium magnets may be dangerous if not handled properly. A domino-sized pair can slam together from more than six inches apart and smash fingers with their magnetic force. It's far easier to slide neodymium magnets apart than it is to pull them apart.

MATERIALS

⊕ Watch Batteries

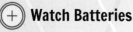 Electrical Tape

 Strong Magnets

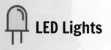 LED Lights

LET'S EXPERIMENT

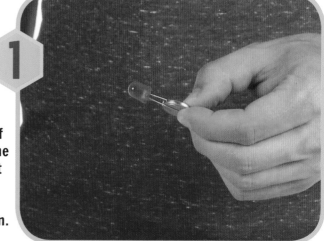

1

PLACE the battery between the two "legs" of the LED. If the LED does not light up, flip the battery and try again.

2

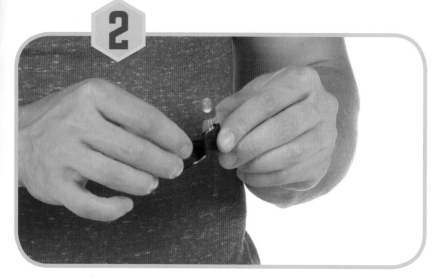

CUT a small piece of electrical tape, then wrap it around the LED legs and battery to secure them together.

3 PLACE a strong magnet on the top of the battery. Cut another piece of tape, then use it to secure the magnet to the battery.

MAKE multiple darts of different colors, then set up a paint can lid or some other metal object as your target (you can even use a permanent marker to draw circles and other scoring areas—just like a dart board!). Turn the lights off, toss the darts at the target and whoever's darts stick closest to the center wins!

4

HOW DOES IT WORK?

A light-emitting diode, or LED, is used when bright, low power and low heat lights are needed. In a diode, electrons rise to and fall from precise energy levels. When an electron falls to a lower energy level, light energy is emitted. It's the size of the fall (the gap) that decides the frequency of the light (i.e. the color of the visible light). What you see, then, is green and blue light, not white light through green or blue plastic.

Did you know?

NICK HOLONYAK JR., AN ENGINEER AT GENERAL ELECTRIC, INVENTED THE FIRST VISIBLE-SPECTRUM LED IN 1962. TODAY, LEDS ARE USED IN TRAFFIC LIGHTS, VEHICLE BRAKE LIGHTS, TELEVISIONS AND MORE!

CENTRIPETAL FORCE BOARD

PUT NEWTON'S FIRST LAW TO THE TEST!

MATERIALS

Rope

Safety Goggles

Water

3 Plastic Cups

Thin Square Board

Square Sheet of Rubber

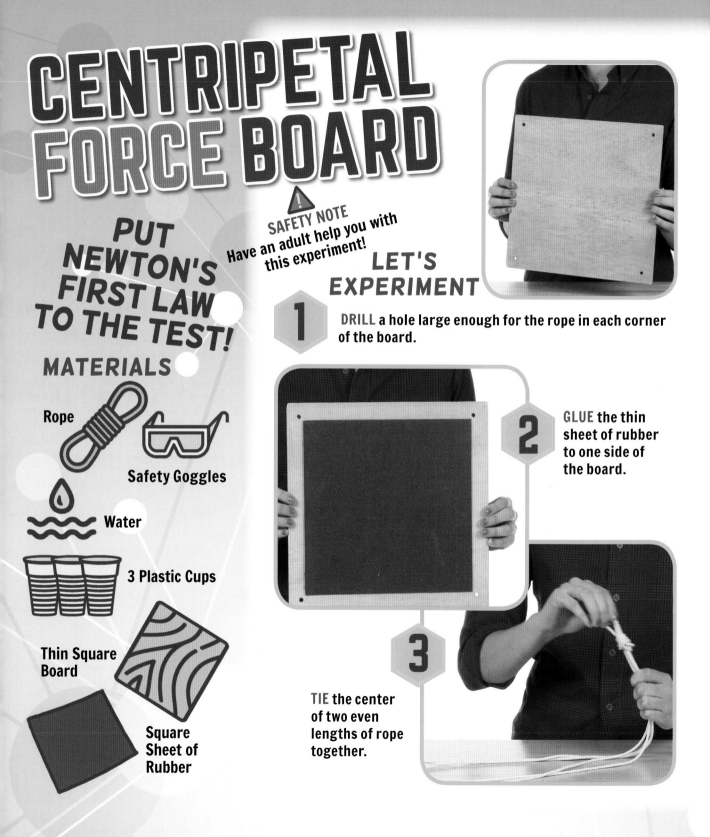

LET'S EXPERIMENT

1 DRILL a hole large enough for the rope in each corner of the board.

2 GLUE the thin sheet of rubber to one side of the board.

3 TIE the center of two even lengths of rope together.

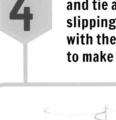

PULL one strand of rope through each hole and tie a knot in each end to keep the rope from slipping back through the hole. Lift the board with the rope where the four strands join together to make sure the length of each strand is even.

PLACE the three plastic cups in the center of the board and fill them with water.

HOW DOES IT WORK?

Any object moving in a circle is experiencing centripetal force. In this case, you are creating the force by swinging the board in a circle. According to Newton's First Law of Motion, objects in motion tend to remain in motion unless acted upon by an external force. Of course, gravity is acting on the water in the glasses and the board, too. But as you continue to swing the board, the glasses "catch" the water each time before it can spill—as long as you swing fast enough, that is. As long as the force of your circular swinging is greater than the force of gravity on the water, you'll stay dry!

SLOWLY begin swinging the board. When you are ready, swing it in a complete circle, then slowly bring the board to a stop.

Did you know?

CENTRIPETAL FORCE IS WHAT KEEPS YOU IN YOUR SEAT ON AN UPSIDE-DOWN ROLLER COASTER!

CD HOVERCRAFT

THIS EXPERIMENT WILL LIFT MORE THAN JUST YOUR SPIRITS!

LET'S EXPERIMENT

MATERIALS

Compact Disc (CD)

Water Bottle Cap (sport-style push/pull closure)

Card Stock

Tack or Pushpin

Balloon

Hot Glue Gun

Scissors

1

USING a pushpin, poke three to four holes around the top of a closed water bottle cap. Make sure the holes go all the way through the plastic of the cap and that the tamper-proof ring is removed so the cap can sit flat on the table.

2

GLUE the cap to the center of the CD (over the hole in the CD) with the glue gun. Don't use too much glue, but be sure there's an airtight seal between the cap and the CD. (Giving the cap a slight twist as you glue it to the CD will help seal it nicely.) Allow the glue to harden and set completely.

3

USING the scissors, take a 8.5-inch by 3-inch piece of cardstock and cut a 2-inch slit about 1 inch from each end. One cut should start on the bottom of the cardstock and the other should start on the top. Bend the cardstock into a circle and slide the upper slit into the lower one to create a paper "collar."

4

5

6

BLOW UP the balloon. Pinch it closed, then twist (do not tie!) the balloon to seal the neck shut to keep the air inside.

PULL the twisted end of the balloon through the collar. Hold the twist in the neck to trap the air and stretch the balloon's opening completely over the bottle cap.

SET your hovercraft on an open, flat surface and untwist the balloon neck. The air escapes from the balloon, lifts the CD a tiny bit and you have a hovercraft gliding effortlessly over the surface!

NOTE: If the hovercraft doesn't slide or spin easily, make sure the CD isn't warped or cracked. You can also check the seal around the CD or poke larger or more holes into the bottle cap.

Did you know?

BRITISH ENGINEER SIR CHRISTOPHER COCKERELL DEVELOPED THE FIRST PRACTICAL HOVERCRAFT IN THE 1950s. TODAY, HOVERCRAFT ARE USED IN MILITARY AND DISASTER RELIEF EFFORTS AS WELL AS FOR RECREATIONAL SPORT.

HOW DOES IT WORK?

Hovercrafts use air to lift a vehicle off of a surface but there has to be a lot of it moving very fast, straight down. As the balloon contracts, air is pushed through the holes you punched in the bottle cap. This air escapes from under the CD in all directions. Due to the shape, smoothness and weight distribution of the rig, the escaping air creates a thin cushion between the CD and the surface. This cushion of air dramatically reduces the friction between the CD and the surface, allowing your hovercraft to move freely.

SODA CAN JUMP

DO YOU KNOW WHAT'S "UP" WITH BERNOULLI'S PRINCIPLE?

MATERIALS

Empty Soda Can

2 Coffee Mugs

LET'S EXPERIMENT

1 PLACE one mug in front of the other.

2 PLACE the empty soda can in one of the mugs.

3

BLOW air between the soda can and mug to make it "jump" into the empty mug. Adjust the distances between the mugs if necessary.

HOW DOES IT WORK?

This is an example of Bernoulli's Principle, the same principle that allows heavier-than-air objects, like airplanes, to fly. Daniel Bernoulli, an 18th-century Swiss mathematician, found that the faster air flows over the surface of something, the less the air pushes on that surface. That means that the air pressure on the object is lower than average.

Blowing air in between the empty can and the first coffee mug creates an area of high pressure between the bottom of the can and the inside of the coffee mug. The harder you blow, the more rapidly the air pressure between the surfaces increases. As the pressure between the surfaces raises, the pressure above the can stays the same, creating a bigger difference in pressure that launches the can up and out, like a jump! The force of gravity causes the can to fall, hopefully into the second mug.

Did you know?

DANIEL BERNOULLI PUBLISHED HIS GROUNDBREAKING FINDINGS ON FLUID MECHANICS IN *HYDRODYNAMICA* IN 1738.

WIND-UP RACER

GET ON A ROLL WITH POTENTIAL AND KINETIC ENERGY!

MATERIALS

Spool

Tape

Washer

Toothpick

Pencil

Rubber Band

Scissors

LET'S EXPERIMENT

1

FEED the rubber band through the spool (a bit of the rubber band should stick out from each end of the spool). You may need to use the toothpick to push or pull it through.

2

BREAK the toothpick so that it is a little smaller than the diameter of the spool, then feed it through one of the rubber band loops. Pull the rubber band taut so that the toothpick lays flat on one end of the spool.

USING the scissors, cut a piece of tape, then tape the toothpick to the end of the spool.

4

ON the other end of the spool, thread the rubber band through the center of a washer.

WIND-UP RACER

5

SLIDE the pencil through the rubber band and wind the pencil. This will twist the rubber band.

6

ONCE the rubber band is wound up, put the spool down on its side on a smooth surface and let go!

TAKE IT FURTHER

Try testing different spool sizes. Which size rolls fastest? Which size rolls the farthest?

HOW DOES IT WORK?

When you twist the rubber band with the pencil, you stretch the rubber band and wind it up. This winding and stretching creates and stores potential energy, energy that has the ability to do work in the future but is not currently performing any work. The more you twist the rubber band, the more potential energy you create. When you put the spool down on a surface, however, the rubber band unwinds and converts the potential energy into kinetic energy, the energy of a moving object, as the spool rolls across the surface.

Did you know?

ALTHOUGH RUBBER BANDS WERE FIRST PATENTED IN 1845, ANCIENT MEXICAN CULTURES CREATED AN EARLY FORM OF RUBBER THOUSANDS OF YEARS AGO BY MIXING MILKY-WHITE TREE SAP (LATEX) WITH JUICES FROM MORNING GLORY VINES.

INERTIA RING

HOW MANY HEX NUTS CAN YOU DROP IN THE BOTTLE?

MATERIALS

Hex Nuts

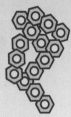

Inertia Ring (make your own using the inner cardboard ring from a roll of masking tape)

1- or 2-Liter Bottle

LET'S EXPERIMENT

1 BALANCE the ring vertically on the mouth of the empty bottle.

2 SET a single hex nut vertically on the ring. Make sure the hex nut is directly centered over the opening of the bottle.

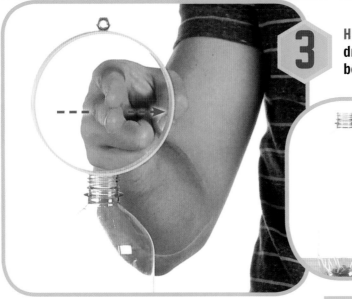

3

HIT OR PULL the ring from its interior. The nut drops straight through the mouth and falls to the bottom of the bottle. See how many you can stack!

TAKE IT FURTHER

Using a cell phone or video camera, record your experiment to playback the finer details in slow motion and observe.

HOW DOES IT WORK?

According to Newton's First Law, an object at rest will remain at rest unless acted on by an outside force. By hitting the ring on its outside, the plastic flexes upward at the same time. That upward flex overcomes the hex nut's stationary inertia, pushing it up and away from the bottle until gravity curves it back down to the table.

However, when you hit the ring on its inside, the plastic flexes downward. The plastic actually drops out from under the hex nut and zips off sideways. Although the hex nut has lost its support, it's not moving due its stationary inertia. Gravity soon overcomes the hex nut's stationary inertia and moves the nut straight down into the bottle. Once it's moving, the hex nut won't stop moving, speed up, slow down or change directions either (due to its moving inertia) unless something–the bottle, your hand, the floor or the ground–gets in the way and causes any of those options to occur.

Did you know?

SIR ISAAC NEWTON
FORMULATED HIS FINDINGS ON INERTIA BASED ON THE WORK OF GALILEO GALILEI, WHO ORIGINALLY DISCOVERED THE CONCEPT OF INERTIA WHILE TRYING TO EXPLAIN THE MOVEMENT OF THE EARTH AROUND THE SUN.

ANTI-GRAVITY WATER

IT'S NOT MAGIC— IT'S SCIENCE!

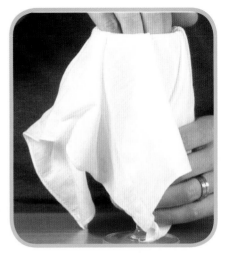

MATERIALS

- Wine Glass
- Handkerchief
- Water
- Pitcher
- Bowl

LET'S EXPERIMENT

1 DRAPE the handkerchief over the glass, then push it down into the center.

2 POUR water into the middle of the handkerchief until the glass is ¾ full with water.

3 PULL the handkerchief down the sides of the glass, making it taut (stretched tightly across the surface of the glass). Grip the ends of the handkerchief at the bottom of the glass in one hand.

READ (AND THINK THROUGH) THIS NEXT PART BEFORE YOU DO IT:

4 **PLACE** one hand over the mouth of the glass, then flip the glass upside down and remove your hand from the mouth of the glass. Do this over the bowl (or a sink) as a few drops may leak out.

5 **GENTLY PULL** the sides of the handkerchief away from the glass. It holds!

HOW DOES IT WORK?

Why doesn't all of the water pour out of the glass when it is inverted? When the handkerchief is tightly stretched across the mouth of the glass, the holes in the fabric become incredibly small. This action allows the water molecules to bond to other water molecules, creating what is called surface tension. The water stays in the glass even though there are tiny holes in the handkerchief because the molecules of water are joined together to form a thin membrane between each opening in the cloth.

SURFACE TENSION IS A FORCE IN THE SURFACE LAYER OF A LIQUID THAT CAUSES IT TO ACT LIKE AN ELASTIC SHEET.

Did you know?

ALTHOUGH USED BY THE GREEKS AND ROMANS, HANDKERCHIEFS BECAME POPULAR AS FASHION ACCESSORIES IN THE 16TH CENTURY. IN FACT, SHAKESPEARE'S TRAGEDY *OTHELLO* FEATURES A HANDKERCHIEF AS A KEY PLOT DEVICE.

MAGIC ROLLBACK CAN

GET ALL WOUND UP WITH KINETIC ENERGY.

MATERIALS

Metal Can (coffee, oats or peanuts cans work well)

Screwdriver

9-Volt Battery

Rubber Band

Tape

2 Paperclips

LET'S EXPERIMENT

1

PLACE the lid on the bottom of the can.

2

USING the screwdriver, have an adult make a hole in the middle of the bottom of the metal can (through the lid and can itself). Be careful around the sharp metal edges that you may create when making the hole. Separate the punctured lid from the can.

3

TAPE the 9-volt battery to the middle of the rubber band. Make sure the rubber band is taped to both sides of the battery just below the terminals.

4

PUSH one end of your rubber band loop through the hole in the bottom of the can. Secure it by attaching one of the paperclips, then tape down the paperclip.

MAGIC ROLLBACK CAN

5 STRETCH the rubber band across the length of the can and push the other end of the rubber band loop through the hole in the lid. Secure the rubber band with a paperclip.

NOTE: The bottom of the battery should NOT touch the can. If it does, try a shorter rubber band.

6 SET the can on its side on a hard surface and give it a roll. Once the can comes to a stop, it begins to roll back to you!

HOW DOES IT WORK?

While the can is rolling, it has kinetic energy. As it slows down, the energy is transferred into potential energy: the twisted rubber band inside the can. As it untwists, the rubber band's potential energy is transferred back to the can as kinetic energy, which is why it rolls!

The secret to all this energy transfer comes from the weight of the 9-volt battery taped to the rubber band inside the can. While the battery is being pulled down by gravity, it is simultaneously subjected to a twisting force from the rubber band. As long as the force being exerted by gravity on the weight is greater than the twisting rubber band's force on the weight (meaning that the weight flips over the rubber band), the rubber band will continue to twist.

Once all of the kinetic energy from the rolling can has been exhausted by converting to heat (friction) or potential energy (the twisted rubber band), the can stops rolling. That's when the weighted rubber band can start to unwind. Because of the weight in the middle of the rubber band, only the ends of the band are able to unwind, and that unwinding creates the force which starts the can rolling backwards!

Did you know?

AS THE WEIGHTED RUBBER BAND UNWINDS, IT APPLIES TORQUE TO THE CAN. TORQUE IS A CIRCULAR OR ROTATIONAL FORCE RATHER THAN LINEAR FORCE.

BOUNCING BUBBLE

MAKE A NO-POP BUBBLE WITH WATER AND DISH SOAP!

MATERIALS

Dish Soap

Water

Clean Cotton Glove

Bubble Wand or Modified Pipette

Cup

NOTE: THIS EXPERIMENT REQUIRES 24 HOURS

LET'S EXPERIMENT

1 **POUR** three parts water and one part dish soap into a small cup.

2 **STIR** to combine. For the best results, let your bubble solution rest for 24 hours.

3 **TEST** the solution with the bubble wand. Blow a bubble and try holding it in your hand. It pops!

PUT the glove on, then blow a bubble. Now try holding the bubble and bouncing it.

TAKE IT FURTHER

Try dipping your ungloved hand in the bubble solution and see how long you can hold the bubble.

HOW DOES IT WORK?

A bubble's worst enemies are oil, dirt and gravity, which when combined can cause a break in the thin soap film of the bubble. The problem with gravity and evaporation is that over time, the water film gets very thin (down to a millionth of an inch) on the outer surface; eventually getting too thin to hold onto itself, the bubble wall collapses completely. A "super" bubble, then, will bounce off of a surface if that surface is free of oil or dirt particles.

Similar to the way we perceive the colors in a rainbow or an oil slick, we see the colors in a bubble through the reflection and the refraction of light waves off the inner and outer surfaces of the bubble wall.

Did you know?

WHILE THE FREEZING POINT OF WATER IS 32 DEGREES FAHRENHEIT, THE FREEZING POINT OF SOAP IS ABOUT 12 DEGREES FAHRENHEIT, WHICH MEANS YOU CAN TRY MAKING FROZEN BUBBLES ON AN ESPECIALLY COLD WINTER DAY!

SQUEEZE ROCKET LAUNCHER

⚠ SAFETY NOTE
Never point the straw rocket at anyone.

A LITTLE THRUST CAN GO A LONG WAY.

LET'S EXPERIMENT

MATERIALS

Squeezable Plastic Bottle with a Narrow Mouth

Modeling Clay or Playdough

2 Straws (one large in diameter and one small; the larger one must be able to slip over the smaller straw)

1 DROP the smaller straw into the opening of the bottle. Leave as much straw as possible sticking out of the bottle to hold up the larger straw.

2 USE modeling clay to create a seal between the smaller straw and the hole in the bottle.

3 CREATE a stopper in the end of the large straw by plugging it with clay.

4

HOLDING the plugged end upright, slide the larger straw over the smaller straw and squeeze or mash the bottle. The larger straw launches off the smaller straw!

HOW DOES IT WORK?

According to Newton's First Law, an object at rest (the larger straw) wants to either stay at rest (if it's not moving) or keep moving in a straight line. The straw will not move unless some force is applied to it. That's where your squeezing comes in. Newton's Third Law says that for every action there is an equal and opposite reaction. As you squeeze the bottle, air is forced out of the smaller straw and pushes against the clay plug in the larger straw. The resulting force causes the straw to "launch" through the air.

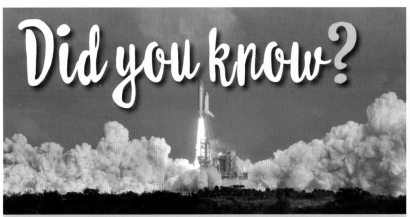

Did you know?

NEWTON'S THIRD LAW EXPLAINS HOW ROCKETS GENERATE THRUST, A PRINCIPLE ENGINEERS ALSO USE WHEN DESIGNING JET ENGINES, MISSILES AND OTHER PROJECTILES. THE MOVEMENT OF AIR MOLECULES CAUSED BY THE COMBUSTION OF FUEL IN AN ENGINE FORCES THE ROCKET TO MOVE.

WATER TWIST

⚠️ SAFETY NOTE
Have an adult help you with this experiment!

GET AN UP-CLOSE LOOK AT THE POWER OF COHESION.

MATERIALS

 Thumbtack

 1-Liter Bottle with Cap

💧 Water

LET'S EXPERIMENT

1 FILL a 1-liter bottle with water and screw on the cap.

2 USING a thumbtack, poke five evenly-spaced holes a few millimeters apart on one side of the bottle, near the bottom, in a line.

3 LOOSEN the cap to release the water and observe the separate streams pouring from the bottle.

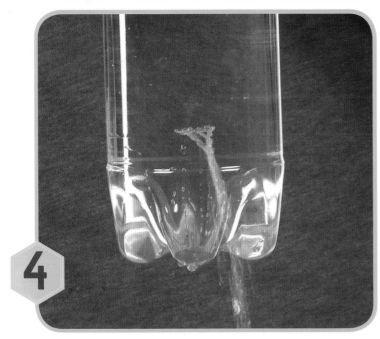

4

RUN your finger left-to-right or horizontally along the streams of water. Observe. Now pass your finger through the streams vertically. What changes?

HOW DOES IT WORK?

When you run your finger horizontally through the streams of water, the force at work is called cohesion. Cohesion happens when molecules of a substance stick to each other. Water is a highly cohesive substance because its molecules are polar: each water molecule consists of one oxygen atom, possessing a weak negative charge, and a pair of hydrogen atoms that sport a slightly positive charge. The negative charge of the oxygen attracts the positive charge of the hydrogen atoms and hydrogen bonds are formed. These bonds are strong enough to create cohesion, but are easily broken when you run your finger vertically over the stream again. On the vertical pass-through, the streams resume their separate flows.

Did you know?

ALTHOUGH WATER COVERS ABOUT 71 PERCENT OF THE EARTH'S SURFACE, ONLY 3.5 PERCENT OF IT IS DRINKABLE.

PING-PONG POPPER

THIS EXPERIMENT WILL SPARK YOUR CURIOSITY AND MORE!

MATERIALS

Car Battery Filler

Punch Awl or Small Phillips Head Screwdriver

Spark Igniter

 Ping-Pong Ball

91% Rubbing Alcohol

LET'S EXPERIMENT

1

UNDO the top of the battery filler and toss the tube aside.

2 HAVE an adult use a punch awl or a Phillips screwdriver to make a hole in the center of the filler.

3 CAREFULLY take apart the spark igniter handle. Remove the nut and washer as well.

4 INSERT the igniter through the opening you created in the filler. Push it through until you can see the threading.

5 REASSEMBLE the igniter. Start by screwing the nut and washer back on. Make sure it's tight! It helps if you hold onto the igniter from the inside.

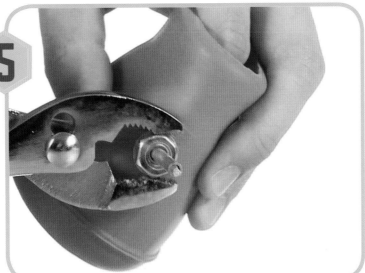

PING-PONG POPPER

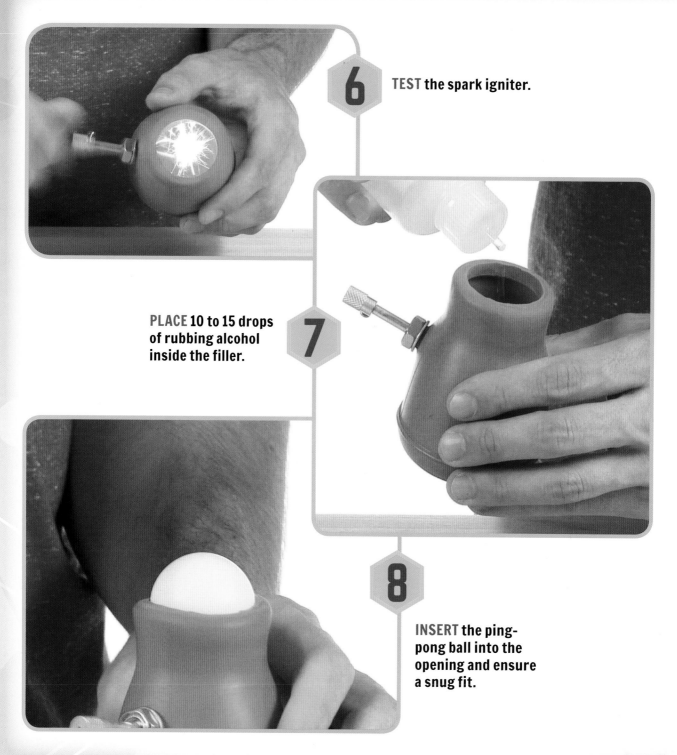

6 TEST the spark igniter.

7 PLACE 10 to 15 drops of rubbing alcohol inside the filler.

8 INSERT the ping-pong ball into the opening and ensure a snug fit.

ROTATE the igniter handle to ignite the rubbing alcohol and shoot out the ping-pong ball. Once you've done that, turn the igniter again to observe the ignition effect inside the filler.

9

IN CASE OF A FIRE INSIDE THE FILLER, COVER THE HOLE WITH A PLATE OR SIMILAR OBJECT.

HOW DOES IT WORK?

The spark igniter ignites the vapors from the rubbing alcohol inside the popper. The resulting combustion causes the air inside the popper to expand rapidly, creating air pressure. When the air pressure finds its way out, this is called the point of least resistance. In this case, the point of least resistance is the seal between the surface of the ping-pong ball and the popper itself. Since the ping-pong ball is tightly squeezed into the popper, it takes a lot of air pressure to dislodge the ping-pong ball due to friction. Once the air pressure exceeds the necessary force to overcome the friction, the force blasts the ball off with a pop!

Did you know?

SPARK IGNITERS *CAN BE FOUND IN GRILLS, LANTERNS, STOVES, GAS FIREPLACES AND JUST ABOUT ANY ITEM THAT REQUIRES A SMALL SPARK TO LIGHT.*

EGG IN A BOTTLE TRICK

LEARN THE SCIENCE BEHIND THIS CLEVER CROWD-PLEASER.

MATERIALS

Erlenmeyer Flask or Glass Juice Bottle

Matches

Birthday Candles

Strips of Paper

2 Hard-Boiled Eggs (slightly larger than the mouth of the flask or bottle)

Vegetable Oil or Shortening

LET'S EXPERIMENT

TO PREPARE, grease the mouth of the flask with vegetable oil.

1 **HAVE** an adult light a match, then use it to light a strip of paper.

2 **QUICKLY** drop the lit strip of paper into the flask, then place an egg on the mouth of the flask. Observe. To get the egg out, tilt the bottle toward your mouth, as if you were about to take a drink, holding the bottle a few inches from your mouth. As the egg rolls forward, blow into the mouth of the bottle without putting your lips against it. The egg should pop back out.

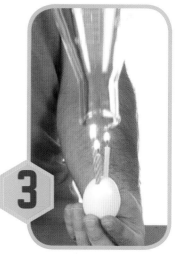

3 **GENTLY** stick three birthday candles in one end of the second egg. Have an adult light the candles.

4 HOLDING the flask upside down, place the egg (candles up) just below the mouth of the flask. Allow the flames to heat up the air inside for just a few seconds, then place the flask down over the candles. The candles will go out and "pop!"—the egg will squeeze up into the bottle!

TAKE IT FURTHER

Try using a small water balloon instead of an egg.

HOW DOES IT WORK?

The burning piece of paper or lit birthday candles heat the air molecules in the bottle, causing the molecules to move far away from each other. Some of the heated molecules escape out past the egg resting on the mouth of the bottle (you see this when the egg starts to wiggle). When the flame eventually dies out, the heated air molecules in the bottle cool down and move closer together, making room for new air molecules. This is what scientists refer to as a partial vacuum. The pressure of the air molecules outside the bottle is so great that it "pushes" the egg into the bottle.

Did you know?

THIS CLASSIC SCIENCE EXPERIMENT IS MORE THAN 100 YEARS OLD. THE ORIGINAL DEMONSTRATION USED A HARD-BOILED EGG AND A GLASS MILK BOTTLE.

HOMEMADE LUNG

⚠️ **HAVE AN ADULT HELP YOU**
with the utility knife in Step 1
and the drill in Step 6!

CREATE A WORKING LUNG SIMULATOR!

MATERIALS

Drill

Straw

Modeling Clay

2 Rubber Bands

Scissors

Utility Knife

Plastic Bottle with Cap

2 Balloons

LET'S EXPERIMENT

1

USE the utility knife to cut off the bottom of the bottle.

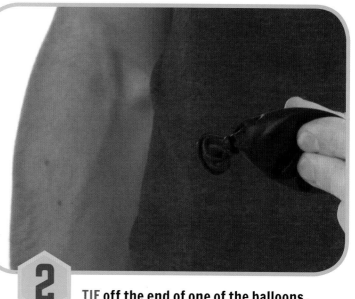

2 TIE off the end of one of the balloons.

3

CAREFULLY use a pair of scissors to cut off the (non-tied) end of the balloon.

4

STRETCH the end of the balloon over the bottom of the bottle, then secure it with a rubber band.

5

INSERT the straw into the end of the untied balloon, securing it with the other rubber band.

HOMEMADE LUNG

6

ASK an adult to help you drill a hole in the center of the bottle cap.

7

PUSH the straw through the bottom of the cap.

8

PUT the balloon-covered end of the straw into the bottle, then screw on the cap.

USE the modeling clay to create a seal around the straw where it exits the bottle cap.

PULL on the end of the balloon that is wrapped around the bottom of the bottle to watch the balloon inside the bottle inflate.

HOW DOES IT WORK?

When the bottle is sealed off by the balloon on one end and the cap, straw and balloon at the other, you create a container that is nearly airtight, meaning air cannot go in or out. By pulling the balloon, you are increasing the volume of the container. However, the volume of air inside the container remains the same. This creates an area of low air pressure inside the bottle, while the air pressure outside the bottle remains the same. The higher air pressure from outside the bottle forces itself into the only opening the bottle has: the straw. Outside air rushes to fill the straw and the connected balloon until the air pressure has balanced. Releasing the balloon takes the container back to its original air pressure and the balloon deflates as air rushes out of the straw.

Did you know?

OUR LUNGS BREATHE IN AS MANY AS 2,400 GALLONS OF AIR EACH DAY. EACH LUNG IS FILLED WITH MILLIONS OF BALLOON-LIKE STRUCTURES CALLED ALVEOLI WHICH SWAP THE CARBON DIOXIDE WASTE IN YOUR BLOOD WITH CLEAN OXYGEN.

OIL AND WATER

SEE HOW NOT ALL LIQUIDS MIX.

LET'S EXPERIMENT

MATERIALS

Vegetable Oil

Water

Food Coloring

2 Glasses with Flat Mouths

Playing Card

NOTE: THIS WILL GET MESSY! DO THIS IN A WASHTUB OR BASIN, OR GO OUTSIDE!

1

FILL the first glass to the brim with vegetable oil.

2

ADD several drops of food coloring in whatever color you like to the second glass, then fill it to the brim with water.

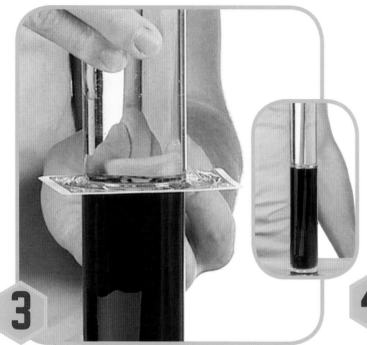

3

SET the playing card over the mouth of the glass filled with vegetable oil and hold it firmly in place. READ THROUGH THIS NEXT PART BEFORE YOU DO IT: Lift the oil glass, turn it upside down, and set it directly on top of the water-filled glass as shown. Slowly and gently remove the playing card. The liquids don't mix!

HOW DOES IT WORK?

Oil and water do not mix because their molecules do not mix—the oil might break up into smaller droplets, but it doesn't truly combine with the water. Also, food coloring mixes with water, but not oil (you might have noticed it does not color the oil at all). If you do see color in the oil, those are tiny droplets of water trapped in the oil.

When you repeat the experiment, however, the oil rises and floats on the surface while the water sinks, because water is heavier (or more dense) than oil. This explains why the oil always stays in the top container.

4

EMPTY the glasses into the sink and repeat the process from Step 1, but when you get to Step 3, turn the glass with colored water upside down and place it on top of the oil-filled glass. Carefully remove the card and watch: the water and oil trade places!

Did you know?

IN CHEMISTRY, FLUIDS THAT ARE CAPABLE OF COMBINING, LIKE WATER AND ALCOHOL, ARE CALLED "MISCIBLE" LIQUIDS. WATER AND OIL, ON THE OTHER HAND, ARE REFERRED TO AS "IMMISCIBLE" LIQUIDS.

KITCHEN SCIENCE

LEARN ABOUT CHEMICAL REACTIONS USING ITEMS YOU CAN FIND IN YOUR PANTRY AND REFRIGERATOR!

SUGAR YEAST BALLOONS

SUGAR CRYSTAL ORNAMENTS

STAINED GLASS SUGAR

See page 160 to learn how to make this colorful treat!

BROWN SUGAR HOMEMADE ICE CREAM

SCIENCE NEVER TASTED SO GOOD!

MATERIALS

 Light Brown Sugar

 2 Zipper-Lock Bags

 Ice

 Measuring Utensils

Large Plastic Container with a Lid

 Rock Salt

 Half-and-Half

 Vanilla Extract (Optional)

LET'S EXPERIMENT

1

FILL the large container about half full with crushed ice and add about 6 tablespoons of rock salt to the ice. Seal the plastic container and shake the ice and salt for about five minutes.

NOTE: You may need to wear your gloves when you're handling the jar, as the rock salt and ice mixture gets down to about 14° F (-10° C).

2

POUR ½ cup of half-and-half, ½ tablespoon brown sugar and 1 teaspoon vanilla extract (if using) into a 1 quart-sized zipper-lock bag and mix well.

3 SEAL the bag tight, allowing as little air to remain in the bag as possible. (Too much air left inside may force the bag open during shaking.) Place the sealed bag inside the other quart-sized bag, again leaving as little air inside as possible, and seal well. Double-bagging helps minimize the risk of salt and ice leaking into the ice cream.

4 PLACE the two bags inside the container with the ice and seal the container.

HOW DOES IT WORK?

Just like when we use salt on icy roads in the winter, salt mixed with ice in this case also causes the ice to melt. When salt comes into contact with ice, the freezing point of the ice is lowered. The lowering of the freezing point depends on the amount of salt added—the more salt added, the lower the temperature will be before the salt-water solution freezes. For example, water will normally freeze at 32° F. A 10 percent salt solution freezes at 20° F, and a 20 percent solution freezes at 2° F.

When salt is added to the ice (or snow), some of the ice melts because the freezing point is lowered. Always remember that heat must be absorbed by the ice for it to melt. The heat that causes the melting comes from the surroundings (the warmer cream mixture). By lowering the temperature at which ice is frozen, you created an environment in which the cream mixture could freeze at a temperature below 32° F into ice cream.

5 SHAKE, rock, roll and mix that container for about 15 to 20 minutes. Once mixed, remove the inner bags from the jar and rinse them well with water. You don't want any salt water accidentally getting into your ice cream. Dry the bags, open and enjoy!

Did you know?

IN 1846, NANCY JOHNSON INVENTED THE HAND-CRANKED ICE CREAM CHURN AND ICE CREAM SURGED IN POPULARITY. THEN, IN 1904, ICE CREAM CONES WERE INVENTED AT THE ST. LOUIS WORLD EXPOSITION WHEN AN ICE CREAM VENDOR RAN OUT OF DISHES AND RESORTED TO USING ROLLED UP WAFFLES TO SERVE HIS SCOOPS INSTEAD!

SOLAR OVEN S'MORES

MELT TREATS IN THE NAME OF SCIENCE!

MATERIALS

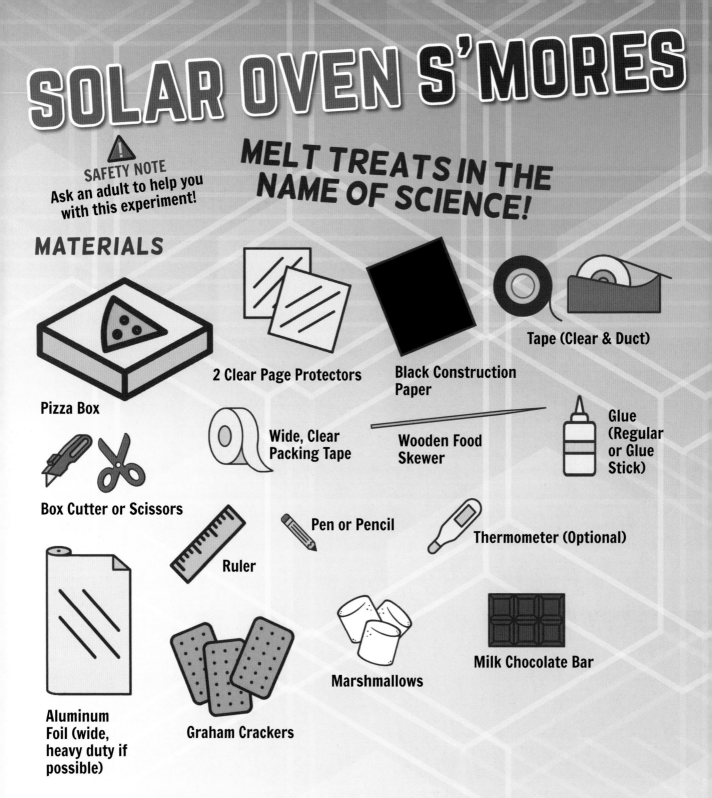

Pizza Box

2 Clear Page Protectors

Black Construction Paper

Tape (Clear & Duct)

Box Cutter or Scissors

Wide, Clear Packing Tape

Wooden Food Skewer

Glue (Regular or Glue Stick)

Ruler

Pen or Pencil

Thermometer (Optional)

Aluminum Foil (wide, heavy duty if possible)

Graham Crackers

Marshmallows

Milk Chocolate Bar

LET'S EXPERIMENT

1

ON THE OUTSIDE of the lid of the pizza box, measure and draw a square about two inches from the four edges of the box. Have an adult cut along the front and two sides of the square using a box cutter or scissors—just don't cut along the hinge side! The square becomes a flap that lifts up on the hinge side in place of the lid.

2

MEASURE and cut a piece of aluminum foil large enough to line the entire bottom and two sides of the pizza box. Be sure to use the foil with the shiny side up. (Note: If you need to join two narrower pieces to do this, fold them together along an edge, then tightly press the seam between them flat.)

3

APPLY glue to the bottom and two sides of the box and lay the foil on top of the glue. Smooth and press the foil so that it sticks in place.

4

MEASURE and cut a piece of black construction paper that's 1 to 2 inches smaller than the bottom of the pizza box (you may need to use more than one piece of paper if the box is large). Center the black paper directly on the foil bottom of the box, then tape down the edges with the clear, wide packing tape.

5

MEASURE and cut a piece of aluminum foil large enough to cover the inside surface of the flap you cut into the lid in Step 1. Cover this surface with glue then smooth and press the foil on the shiny side out.

SOLAR OVEN S'MORES

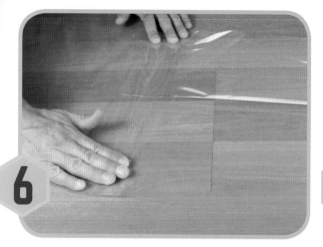

6 GRAB the page protectors and carefully pull the thin sheets apart along the short bottom edge of each sheet. Lay out both sheets and tape their two long edges together to make a single large plastic sheet.

7 TAPE the plastic sheet to the inside of the box lid so that it's smooth and tight. DON'T tape it to the flap you cut out; tape it inside the lid. The flap should still move freely and the plastic should cover the flap's opening from underneath the lid.

8 WRAP a five-inch piece of tape around the skewer near its flat end. Leave enough loose tape on both sides so that the skewer looks like a "T." Tape it to the side of the flap next to the dents you made in the lid in Step 8. This will be the "kickstand" for the lid.

9 USE the sharp end of the skewer to poke two small dents about two inches apart into one side of the lid. Make them about half an inch from the flap and about halfway along the flap. Don't poke all the way through—these dents are a way to prop the flap open during cooking. (See Step 11.)

10 OPEN the lid and load your oven with a few s'mores. To make a s'more, use one graham cracker as a "pan" to hold the chocolate and the marshmallow, then top with another graham cracker. Keep the s'mores somewhat spread out on the black paper. Close the lid.

HOW DOES IT WORK?

While a true oven can reach temperatures far above the heat trapped inside a pizza box, your "solar oven," or solar cooker, works on the principle of collecting heat energy and retaining or directing it for cooking. You cover as much of the interior of the box as possible with reflective material (in this case, aluminum) in order to direct as much heat as possible into the center of the cooker. Meanwhile, the actual "cooking" surface is black construction paper because black retains heat very well. As heat is retained, the air inside the oven also heats up and the plastic helps hold it in the small space.

11

TAKE IT FURTHER

GO OUT into the midday sunshine, set your box in a spot that will have full sun for a long time and open the reflective flap. Adjust the flap to reflect as much light (heat) as possible into the oven. You'll have to leave it for a while, but check on it every so often to make sure it's getting maximum sunlight. Depending on the weather, your treats will be ready in about 30 to 90 minutes!

Try making a few s'mores with dark or white chocolate. Which chocolate melts fastest? Why do you think that is?

SUGAR YEAST BALLOONS

LEARN HOW TO GET A RISE OUT OF YEAST.

LET'S EXPERIMENT

MATERIALS

Granulated Sugar

4 Empty 1-Liter Bottles

4 Soda Bottle Caps

4 Balloons (Same Size)

4 Yeast Packets

Measuring Cup and Spoons

Funnel

Very Warm Water

1 MEASURE and pour 8 ounces of very warm water into each 1-liter bottle.

NOTE: The water must be between 100 and 110 degrees Fahrenheit.

2 STICK the funnel in the mouth of one bottle, then add a packet of yeast to the bottle. Repeat this step for the remaining three bottles using the three remaining yeast packets.

3 TO THE second bottle, add 1 teaspoon of sugar. Add 2 teaspoons of sugar to the third bottle, then add 3 teaspoons of sugar to the fourth bottle. Do not add any sugar to the first bottle.

0tsp   1tsp   2tsp   3tsp

4

CAP each bottle and shake well.

5

REMOVE the bottle caps, then stretch one balloon over the mouth of each bottle. Let the bottles sit for several hours. Observe. Which balloon inflates the most? The least? Why do you think that is?

HOW DOES IT WORK?

Yeasts are single-celled fungi that feed on sugar. Adding the sugar to the warm water yeast solution activates the yeast; as the microorganisms chow down on the sugar, they release carbon dioxide (CO_2). This gas fills the bottles and eventually causes the balloons to expand, allowing you to see the results. If you've ever eaten bread, evidence of this gas is present in the form of countless holes within each slice. But don't worry—the yeast dies off during the baking process.

Did you know?

CERTAIN TYPES OF YEAST (STRAINS OF SACCHAROMYCES CEREVISIAE) ARE ALSO USED TO MAKE BEER AND WINE. IN NATURE, YEAST CAN BE FOUND IN SOILS, AND FLOWER NECTAR AND ON PLANTS, VEGETABLES, FRUITS AND WILD HERBS.

153

FLOATING EGG

WHAT MAKES THE EGG BUOYANT?

MATERIALS

2 Drinking Glasses

2 Raw Eggs

Table Salt

Spoon

LET'S EXPERIMENT

1 FILL one of the drinking glasses almost to the top with plain tap water. Gently drop one of the eggs into the water-filled glass. It sinks right to the bottom!

2 FILL the second drinking glass half-full with water. Add 4 tablespoons of table salt to the water and stir. Fill the rest of the cup with water, almost to the top.

3

GENTLY PLACE the second egg into the saltwater solution. It floats!

TAKE IT FURTHER

Try using different amounts of salt to see how high or low you can make the egg float!

HOW DOES IT WORK?

When submerged in water, the egg sinks because it has a greater density than water. But when you add salt to the water, it increases the density of the solution. Eventually, when enough salt is added to the water, the density of the saltwater becomes greater than the egg's, and the egg floats! The denser the liquid, the easier it is for eggs (and other objects) to float in it. The egg sinks a bit through the top portion of water, the part that is least-mixed, and will rest where it meets the well-mixed dense saltwater.

Did you know?

LOCATED BETWEEN ISRAEL AND JORDAN, AN INLAND LAKE KNOWN AS THE DEAD SEA IS ONE OF THE SALTIEST BODIES OF WATER IN THE WORLD, SO MUCH SO THAT NO ANIMALS OR PLANTS CAN BE FOUND LIVING IT IN, HENCE ITS "DEAD" MONIKER. RATHER THAN SWIM, VISITORS TO THE DEAD SEA FLOAT EFFORTLESSLY DUE TO ITS SALINITY.

SUGAR CRYSTAL ORNAMENTS

MAKE YOUR OWN ROCK CANDY ART FOR THE HOLIDAYS!

SAFETY NOTE
Have an adult help you with this experiment!

NOTE: THIS EXPERIMENT REQUIRES 1 WEEK

MATERIALS

- Granulated Sugar
- Water
- Pipe Cleaners
- Pencil
- Food Coloring
- Glass Jar
- Parchment Paper
- Microwave-Safe Glass (Like Pyrex®)

LET'S EXPERIMENT

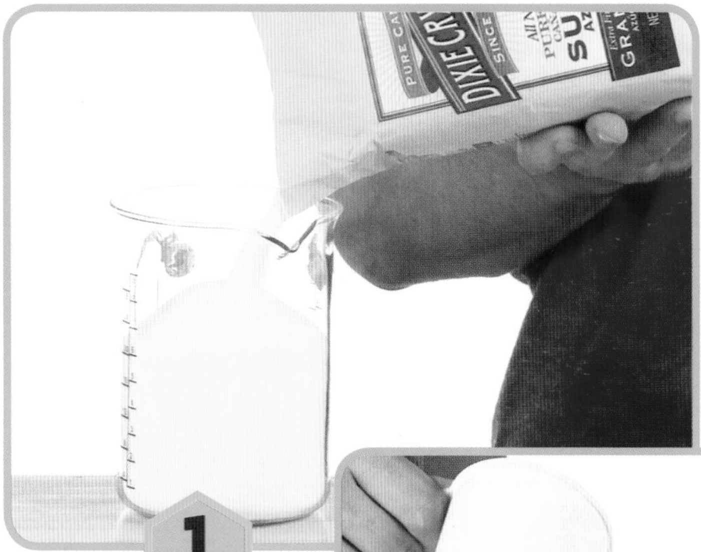

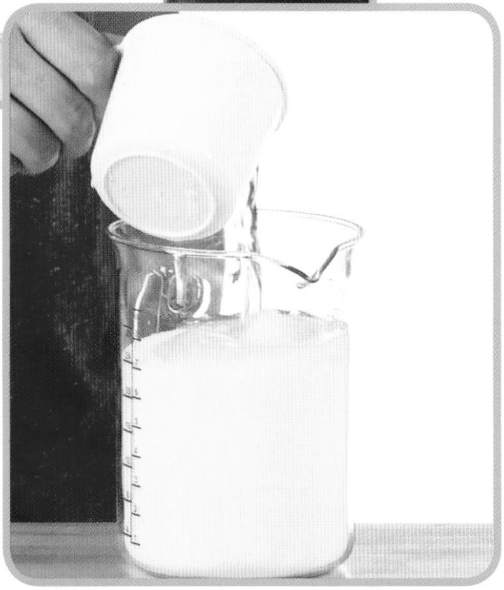

1 **POUR** 3 cups of sugar into a microwave safe container. Add 1 cup of water to the sugar and stir.

2 **WITH** an adult's help, microwave your solution on high for 2 minutes. Use caution when removing the solution from the microwave as it will be extremely hot. Stir it again.

3 MICROWAVE the solution for an additional 2 minutes on high, stirring afterwards.

4

ADD several drops of food coloring, then stir the solution. Transfer the solution into a smaller glass jar. Allow the solution to cool to room temperature.

5 CREATE an ornament shape using pipe cleaners. Wrap the end of the pipe cleaner around the center of a pencil. Dip your ornament into the solution.

SUGAR CRYSTAL ORNAMENTS

6

LAY your ornament on a sheet of parchment paper to dry.

7

PLACE the dried ornament back into the solution carefully, avoiding the side and bottom of the jar. Allow the solution and ornament to sit for at least one week.

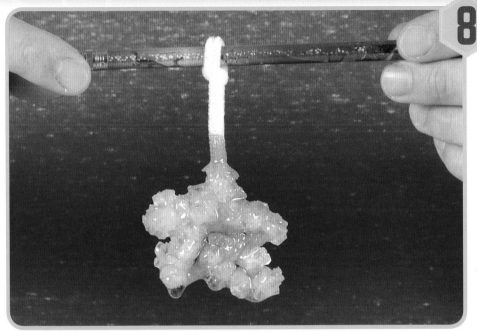

8

PULL the ornament out of the jar and let it dry on the parchment paper.

TAKE IT FURTHER

To make rock candy you can eat, simply swap out the pipe cleaner for a new, clean string. Yum!

HOW DOES IT WORK?

When you mixed the sugar with the water, then heated and stirred the solution repeatedly, you created a supersaturated solution.

A supersaturated solution means that there are far more dissolved particles of solute (the sugar) than the solvent (the water) can usually dissolve and hold at a given temperature. Once you reach the boiling point, you're able to dissolve as much sugar into the water as possible, due to the microscopic expansion of the water molecules.

Dipping your ornament into the solution and allowing it to dry creates a small layer of sugar crystals around the pipe cleaner. These crystals dissolve in the solution, but the pipe cleaner gives them a surface they can use to recrystallize. This small layer is made up of "seed" crystals. Over the course of a week, as sugar particles begin to settle (the precipitate), you can really see just how much sugar has crystallized on your ornament!

Did you know?

THE WORD CANDY COMES FROM THE ARABIC "QANDĪ," WHICH IS DERIVED FROM THE SANSKRIT WORD "KHAṆDA." SINCE SANSKRIT IS ONE OF THE OLDEST LANGUAGES IN THE WORLD, THIS MEANS CANDIED TREATS HAVE BEEN AROUND FOR QUITE SOME TIME.

STAINED GLASS SUGAR

IT'S EDIBLE AND EDUCATIONAL!

MATERIALS

Granulated Sugar

Food Coloring

Stovetop Safe Container (Like Pyrex®) or Saucepan

Cream of Tartar

Candy Thermometer

Light Corn Syrup

Measuring Cups and Spoons

Shallow Aluminum Baking Pan

Metal Utensils (Spoon, Fork and Knife)

Non-Stick Cooking Spray

Cooking Mitt

Water

LET'S EXPERIMENT

1

COMBINE 1¾ cups granulated sugar, 1 cup water, ½ cup light corn syrup and ⅛ teaspoon cream of tartar in a stovetop safe container or saucepan. Stir the solution. Slowly heat the mixture to a low boil while stirring to prevent the sugar from caramelizing.

2

KEEP the mixture at a low boil and add a candy thermometer to the mixture.

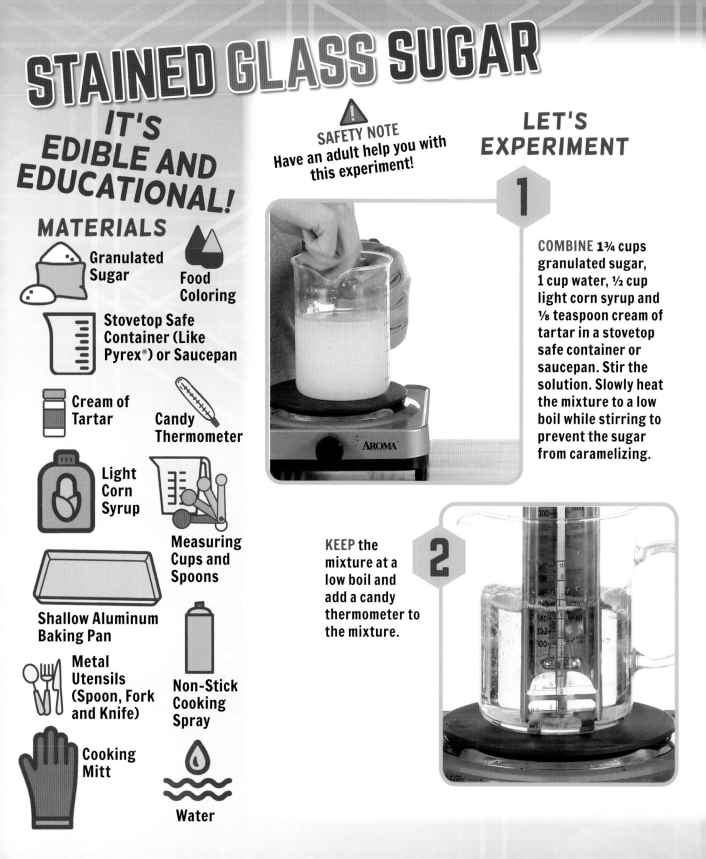

3 COAT the aluminum foil pan with cooking spray.

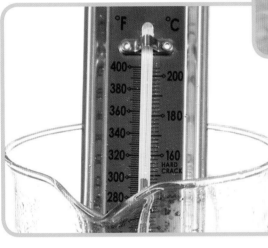

4 KEEP an eye on the thermometer. When the temperature reaches 300 degrees Fahrenheit, turn off the heat. Using an oven mitt, carefully remove the container or saucepan.

5 HAVE an adult use the oven mitt to carefully and quickly pour the solution into the aluminum foil pan. Careful—it's HOT!

STAINED GLASS SUGAR

ADD drops of food coloring as desired.

6

7

USE a spoon to drag and swirl the food coloring throughout the foil pan. Let cool completely.

8

CAREFULLY **remove the Stained Glass Sugar from the foil pan by gently flipping it over. Bon appétit!**

HOW DOES IT WORK?

Stained Glass Sugar, or sugar glass, is created when you dissolve sugar in water and heat it to 300-310 degrees Fahrenheit (149-154 degrees Celsius). This is called the "hard crack" stage of candy making. You've made what a chef calls a reduction by boiling away excess water to concentrate flavors and ingredients. As the water boils off, both the temperature and the sugar concentration rise. At this point of heating, the sugar concentration in the syrup is about 99 percent.

Since sugar dissolved in water will normally crystallize back to sugar again, the addition of the corn syrup to the solution prevents this from happening by holding the dissolved sugar molecules in suspension in the solution. Cream of tartar separates the original, complex sugar crystals into glucose and fructose, sugar's simpler components. Adding food coloring prior to hardening creates the "stained glass" look you wanted. Light passing through the translucent sugar glass will show off the colors and patterns you spread around in it.

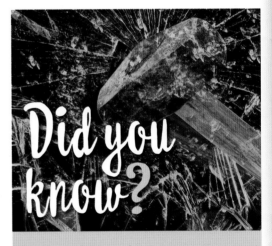

Did you know?

SUGAR GLASS CAN LOOK AND BREAK LIKE REAL GLASS, WHICH IS WHY IT'S SOMETIMES USED IN FILMS AND TV SHOWS IN SCENES WHERE GLASS IS BROKEN. IT'S MUCH CHEAPER TO USE AND REPLACE FOR MULTIPLE TAKES.

GROWING & SHRINKING EGG

GET AN UP-CLOSE LOOK AT OSMOSIS IN ACTION.

MATERIALS

 Karo Corn Syrup

 Water

 Distilled White Vinegar

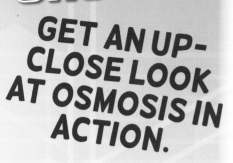 2 Raw Eggs

2 Glasses

 **NOTE: THIS EXPERIMENT REQUIRES 48 HOURS**

LET'S EXPERIMENT

1 FILL both glasses at least half-full with vinegar. Place one egg in each of the glasses.

2 ALLOW the eggs to soak for 24 hours.

REMOVE each egg from its glass. You will be left with the membrane, but no shell!

4

CLEAN the glasses out. Fill one glass half-full with Karo corn syrup. Fill the other glass half-full with water.

GROWING & SHRINKING EGG

5

PLACE one "naked" egg inside each glass, making sure the eggs are completely submerged. Allow the eggs to soak for 24 hours.

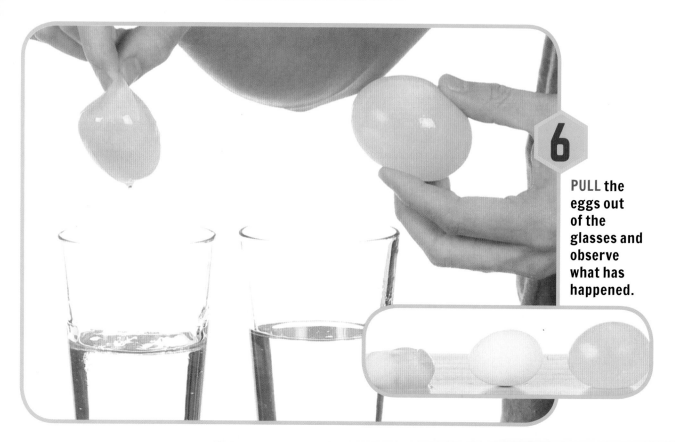

6

PULL the eggs out of the glasses and observe what has happened.

HOW DOES IT WORK?

Vinegar is an acetic acid, and white vinegar from the grocery store is usually about 4 percent acetic acid and 96 percent water. Eggshells are made up of calcium carbonate. The acetic acid in the vinegar reacts with the calcium carbonate in the eggshell to make calcium acetate plus water and carbon dioxide (CO_2), which you see as bubbles on the surface of the shell. When the shell is gone, the egg appears translucent. All that remains is the thin membrane called a semipermeable membrane.

The egg soaking in water expanded because water traveled through the egg's membrane in an effort to equalize the concentration of water on both sides of the membrane. This flow of water through a semipermeable membrane is called osmosis.

Place your naked egg in a glass filled with corn syrup, however, and the egg shrivels up. Since corn syrup has a lower concentration of water than an egg does, the water in the egg moves through the membrane and into the corn syrup to equalize the water concentration levels on both sides, causing the egg to contract and shrink.

TAKE IT FURTHER

Try this experiment with organic or free-range eggs. Do those eggs have eggshells that are stronger or weaker than generic eggs? What about fresh eggs compared to those that have been around for a while?

Did you know?

IN 1979, A CHICKEN AT THE UNIVERSITY OF MISSOURI SET A GUINNESS WORLD RECORD BY LAYING A WHOPPING 371 EGGS IN ONE YEAR!

GLOSSARY

ADHESION
The attraction of like molecules to molecules of a different type.

AMPLITUDE
A way to measure a sound or light wave. Amplitude describes the height of a wave on a graph.

ATMOSPHERIC PRESSURE
The force exerted by air.

ATOMS
The smallest units of ordinary matter that make up a chemical element.

BOILING POINT
The temperature at which a liquid boils. Water's boiling point is 212 degrees F (100 degrees C).

BUOYANCY
The upward force on an object created by a surrounding gas or liquid.

CARBON DIOXIDE
A colorless, odorless gas composed of carbon and oxygen.

CATALYST
A substance that causes or speeds up a chemical reaction yet remains unchanged.

CENTRIPETAL FORCE
A force that pushes an object along a circular path.

CIRCUIT
A complete (or closed) path through which electricity flows.

COHESION
The attraction of like molecules to one another.

CONDUCTOR
A material that permits the flow of an electric current.

CRYSTALLIZATION
The process by which atoms in a liquid or gas form a highly organized structure while becoming a solid.

DENSITY
A measure of how compact a substance is. Density equals mass divided by volume.

DISSOLVE
To become incorporated in liquid, forming a solution.

DRAG
A force caused by friction that slows a moving object. One of the four forces of flight.

ELECTRODE
The parts of a conductor where the electrical current enters and leaves the conductor.

ELECTRON
A negatively charged subatomic particle. Electrons carry electricity.

EXPERIMENT
A scientific procedure done to test a hypothesis or demonstrate a known fact.

FORCE
An influence that changes the motion of a body.

FREEZING POINT
The temperature at which a liquid becomes a solid. Water freezes at 32 degrees F (0 degrees C).

FRICTION
The resistance that occurs when one object moves over another.

FRUCTOSE
A naturally-occurring, highly water-soluble simple sugar found in flowers, berries and root vegetables.

GAS
A substance in a state that has no fixed shape or volume and will expand to fill whatever container it is in.

GEODE
A hollow, spherical rock that has an internal cavity which is usually lined with crystallized quartz and banded agate.

GLUCOSE
A naturally-occurring simple sugar that comes from the food you eat and is absorbed into the bloodstream. The body converts carbohydrates into glucose and uses it as an energy source.

GRAVITY
The force that attracts everything to the center of the Earth, or any other body with mass.

HYDROPHILIC
Tending to mix with or dissolve in water.

HYDROPHOBIC
Tending to repel water.

IMPLOSION
The action of an object violently collapsing in on itself.

INERTIA
The tendency of an object to either stay at rest or remain in motion.

KINETIC ENERGY
The energy of motion; potential energy is converted into kinetic energy as it is used.

LED
Light-Emitting Diode. A semiconductor device that gives off light when an electric force (a current) passes through it in one direction.

LIFT
An upward force caused by differences in air pressure. One of the four forces of flight.

GLOSSARY

LIQUID
A substance that flows freely but has constant volume.

MAGMA
Molten liquid rock located beneath the surface of the Earth.

MAGNETIC FIELD
The area around a magnet which carries the force of magnetism.

MASS
A measure of the amount of matter in an object.

MEMBRANE
A thin layer of cells or tissue that acts as a boundary within an organism.

MOLECULE
The smallest unit of a chemical compound that can be part of a chemical reaction.

NEUTRON
A subatomic particle that does not carry an electric charge.

NEWTON'S FIRST LAW OF MOTION
Objects at rest tend to stay at rest and objects in motion tend to stay in motion, unless an outside force acts upon them.

NEWTON'S THIRD LAW OF MOTION
Every action has an equal and opposite reaction.

NON-NEWTONIAN FLUID
A substance that behaves like a liquid or a solid depending on whether or not it is subjected to force.

OOBLECK
A non-Newtonian fluid made of cornstarch and water.

OSMOSIS
The movement of water molecules passing through a semipermeable membrane from a less concentrated solution into a more concentrated solution.

PENDULUM
A free-swinging weight suspended by a pivot originally used for timekeeping.

POTENTIAL ENERGY
The stored energy an object has because of its position or state.

PRESSURE
A continuous force exerted on an object.

PROTON
A subatomic particle with a positive electric charge.

REACTION
A chemical process in which two or more substances change one another into different substances.

REFRACTION
The process by which light waves bend as they pass through mediums with different densities.

SOLID
A substance with a constant shape and volume.

SOLUBLE
Able to be dissolved in water. Something dissolved in water is called a solute.

SOLVENT
The liquid in which a solute is being dissolved.

STALACTITE
Icicle-like formations found hanging in caves caused by minerals slowly leaking and dripping from the ceiling over the course of many years.

STALAGMITE
Mound-like formations found growing in caves caused by the gradual deposit of minerals dripping onto the cave floor over the course of many years.

SURFACE TENSION
A force in the surface layer of a liquid that causes it to act like an elastic sheet. This is caused by cohesion.

TEMPERATURE
A degree of heat or cold that can be measured with a thermometer.

THERMOMETER
A tool used for measuring temperature.

THERMOREGULATION
The process by which an organism maintains a stable internal body temperature.

THRUST
The force that propels an object (like an aircraft) forward. One of the four forces of flight.

TORQUE
A circular or rotational (rather than linear) force.

VERDIGRIS
A bluish-green coating that forms on the surface of brass, bronze or copper that has been exposed to the elements and has begun to oxidize.

VOLUME
The amount of space taken up by an object.

VORTEX
A spinning, rotating column of fluid aligned along a straight or curved axis.

WEIGHT
The force exerted by gravity on an object. One of the four forces of flight.

STEVE SPANGLER—the very definition of a lifelong learner—first tested out his own experiments as a science teacher in Colorado in the early 1990s. By 2005, he shared his signature fun-filled, unconventional approach with millions by releasing his Mentos Diet Coke Experiment video on YouTube, in which he turned an ordinary bottle of diet soda into an erupting geyser with the addition of Mentos candies. Today, Spangler's ever-growing catalogue of exciting science videos across social media platforms like YouTube, Facebook and Instagram have garnered a whopping one billion combined views, all the better to reach inquisitive minds and inspire them with a love of all things science.

As a bestselling author, educator and television host, Spangler has dedicated his life to getting students hooking on learning and showing them the myriad joys of pursuing STEM-based careers. With more than 1,500 television appearances and multiple Emmy awards under his belt, he has also been dubbed "America's Science Teacher" by Ellen DeGeneres. In fact, Spangler's been a beloved regular guest on *The Ellen DeGeneres Show* more than 20 times, where he has always managed to get the crowd fired up for more (sometimes literally). Aside from hosting his fun television series *DIY Sci*, in which he shows viewers how to use ordinary household items to create thrilling at-home science experiments, Spangler was inducted into the National Speaker Hall of Fame in 2010 and holds a Guinness World Record for conducting the world's largest science experiment in 2009. He is the author of three bestselling science books for kids, including *Smithsonian 10-Minute Science Experiments*, *Naked Eggs and Flying Potatoes* and *Fire Bubbles and Exploding Toothpaste*.

To learn more, visit *SteveSpangler.com*.

Media Lab Books
For inquiries, call 646-838-6637

Copyright 2021 Topix Media Lab

Published by Topix Media Lab
14 Wall Street, Suite 4B
New York, NY 10005

Printed in China

ISBN-13: 978-1-948174-72-5
ISBN-10: 1-948174-72-3

CEO Tony Romando

Vice President & Publisher Phil Sexton
Senior Vice President of Sales & New Markets Tom Mifsud
Vice President of Retail Sales & Logistics Linda Greenblatt
Director of Finance Vandana Patel
Manufacturing Director Nancy Puskuldjian
Financial Analyst Matthew Quinn
Digital Marketing & Strategy Manager Elyse Gregov

Chief Content Officer Jeff Ashworth
Director of Editorial Operations Courtney Kerrigan
Creative Director Steven Charny
Photo Director Dave Weiss
Executive Editor Tim Baker

Content Editor Juliana Sharaf
Art Director Susan Dazzo
Senior Editor Trevor Courneen
Copy Editor & Fact Checker Tara Sherman

The experiments presented herein were originally featured on Steve Spangler's Sick Science YouTube channel.

1C-L21-2